T0303768

One Day in
the Season
of Rain

Sudha Sharma as Mallika and Om Shivpuri as Kalidas in the 1962 production for the
National School of Drama

One Day in the Season of Rain

MOHAN RAKESH

*Translated from the Hindi
with an Introduction, an Afterword, and Notes by*
Aparna Dharwadker and Vinay Dharwadker

PENGUIN BOOKS
An imprint of Penguin Random House

PENGUIN BOOKS

USA I Canada I UK I Ireland I Australia
New Zealand I India I South Africa I China I Singapore

Penguin Books is part of the Penguin Random House group of companies
whose addresses can be found at global.penguinrandomhouse.com

Published by Penguin Random House India Pvt. Ltd
4th Floor, Capital Tower 1, MG Road,
Gurugram 122 002, Haryana, India

First published in Hindi as *Ashadh ka ek din* by Rajpal and Sons, Delhi 1958
This English translation first published by Penguin Books India 2015

Translation, introduction, afterword, and notes copyright © Aparna Dharwadker
and Vinay Dharwadker 2015

Portions of the Introduction excerpted from Aparna Dharwadker, *Theatres of
Independence: Drama, Theory, and Urban Performance in India since 1947*,
University of Iowa Press © 2005. Used with permission.
Portions of the Introduction excerpted from Aparna Dharwadker, 'Mohan Rakesh,
Modernism, and the Postcolonial Present', *South Central Review* 25(1): 147, 151,
152–53 © South Central Review 2008. Reprinted with permission of Johns
Hopkins University Press.

Page 273 is an extension of the copyright page

10 9 8 7 6 5 4 3 2

ISBN 9780670088027

Typeset in Dante MT by R. Ajith Kumar, New Delhi
Printed at Replika Press Pvt. Ltd, India

www.penguin.co.in

This is a legitimate digitally printed version of the book and therefore might not
have certain extra finishing on the cover.

In memory of
Premanand Purshottam Dharwadker
(1925–2013)

I turn from a page
and see his eyes
			watching, mirroring
			whole landscapes of buildings

Contents

Contents

Preface

One Day in the Season of Rain is our new English translation of Mohan Rakesh's Hindi play, *Ashadh ka ek din* (1958), authorized by the writer's estate. Among the plays written in the Indian languages after Independence, *Ashadh* was the first to create a sustained 'buzz' in literary, critical, and theatrical networks at the national level when it entered the spheres of print and performance. Between its two quick editions in the late 1950s and its trendsetting productions in the early 1960s, it established a fresh paradigm for contemporary urban theatre in the new nation, opening the way to the artistically vibrant economy of drama and performance that has come to define a multilingual 'national postcolonial tradition' since then. Over the past five and a half decades, theatre groups and institutions in India and abroad have invested in eighteen notable productions of the play, but its distinguished history as theatre and as literature has not secured its place as yet in the global canon of modernist drama. *Ashadh* is the only original dramatic work in the twentieth century that is a full-scale imaginative exploration of a classical writer's life and texts—an experimental, theatrical equivalent of a

Künstlerroman which, in this case, takes the classical Sanskrit poet Kalidas in his maturity as its extraordinary subject. This book seeks to give Rakesh's play and its aesthetic and cultural legacy the cosmopolitan form that will make them fully accessible to readers, viewers, and performers around the world.

Given its exceptional interplay of text and context, we have positioned our translation in a structure that contains several layers and serves several ends. The book opens with Aparna Dharwadker's general Introduction, which maps out the entire terrain of *Ashadh*, its author's career, its various intertexts, its performance history, and its place in postcolonial modernism. The Introduction is followed by a Map that displays the basic classical and modern geography of *Ashadh*; a comprehensive Chronology of Mohan Rakesh's life, work, and afterlife as a writer (the first such compilation for any modern Indian playwright); and a Translators' Note that explains our treatment of the play, in theory as well as practice. Placed at the centre of the volume, the translation is followed by Vinay Dharwadker's Afterword, which analyses Rakesh's dramatic techniques, his use of classical sources, and his representation of the classical period of Indian literary history. The book then closes with Appendices consisting of short documents (translated from Hindi, also for the first time) that record Rakesh's prospective and retrospective authorial commentary on *Ashadh*; with Notes that include general information, dramaturgical suggestions, and annotations to the play; and with Endnotes and a list of Works Cited.

On a more practical level of organization, our scholarly apparatus utilizes the system of short endnotes, with full bibliographical information provided in the Works Cited. We have simplified the transcription of Indian-language terms and their spelling in English for a twenty-first-century international audience, and have explained our method in the General Notes. To avoid unnecessary duplication, we have listed a large number of publications in the Chronology that do not reappear in the Works Cited; readers should consult the two together for comprehensive coverage of materials by and on Rakesh in print and other media. We have designed the translation to be as self-sufficient as possible; for many readers, our English version needs no annotation, but for some it requires limited explication, which is provided in the Explanatory and Dramaturgical Notes at the end.

Our first debts in this book are to Anita Rakesh, Mohan Rakesh's literary executor, for authorizing a new translation of *Ashadh ka ek din*; and to Neil Scharnick, assistant professor of theatre at Carthage College (Kenosha, Wisconsin), for commissioning it. As a doctoral candidate in the Department of Theatre and Drama at the University of Wisconsin–Madison, Neil read the play in a graduate seminar taught by Aparna in autumn 2008, and developed a strong interest in producing it at Carthage in a new translation. We received Anitaji's permission to translate the play in spring 2009, completed our collaborative translation that autumn, and had the pleasure of watching it come alive on stage in March 2010. A measure of the quality of the Carthage production was its selection for the Regional Competition of the Kennedy Center's annual American College Theater Festival, held at Michigan State University (East Lansing, Michigan) in January 2011. We would like to thank Neil for his confident artistry as director, the cast for their subtle performances, and the crew for an elegant set—complete with a lifelike fawn and real rain on stage! As our translation evolved from text to performance with this production, it reaffirmed the status of *Ashadh ka ek din* as a contemporary stage classic in another language and another setting, and future productions undoubtedly will benefit from the outcomes of that experience.

We are grateful to R. Sivapriya, our commissioning editor at Penguin Books India, New Delhi, who read the draft translation in 2011, and enthusiastically pursued its transition from performance to print. We are equally grateful to our editors Ambar Chatterjee and Richa Burman and their colleagues at Penguin for their remarkable skills in the craft of making books. We would also like to thank our University's Graduate School and its Research Committee, which provided a grant for our collaboration in summer 2014, enabling us to prepare the full manuscript for press. In a wider context, our work has benefited at every stage from Dr Jaidev Taneja's meticulous labour, over three decades, in organizing Mohan Rakesh's papers and making them available to readers worldwide in a succession of invaluable posthumous publications, now gathered into the monumental thirteen-volume *Mohan rakesh rachanavali* (The Works of Mohan Rakesh) under his editorship. We are especially grateful to him for taking the time to respond to queries that only he could have answered. We would also like to celebrate three directors who put *Ashadh ka ek din* on the national map—Shyamanand Jalan, Ebrahim Alkazi, and Satyadev Dubey—and two actors—Om Shivpuri and Sudha Shivpuri—who delivered virtuoso lead performances in all three of Rakesh's full-length plays early in the plays' history. The creative and critical energy that readers, critics, scholars, and theatre professionals have invested in Rakesh over half a century is reciprocally sustained by his astonishing talents as a writer in several genres—he himself remains as vital a presence today as he was during his mercurial lifetime.

Aparna would like to acknowledge the University of Iowa Press for permission to reprint excerpts from Chapter 7 of her book, *Theatres of Independence: Drama, Theory, and Urban Performance in India Since 1947* (2005); and the Johns Hopkins University Press for permission to reprint material from her essay 'Mohan Rakesh, Modernism, and the Postcolonial Present', in *South Central Review* 25.1 (2008), pp. 132–62. In addition, Anita Rakesh's gracious permission has allowed us to include two important documents in our Appendices: a selection of entries about *Ashadh* from Mohan Rakesh's Diary (1985); and an excerpt from Rakesh's letter of 7 August 1958 to Upendranath Ashk, which discussed the play with a fellow writer and close friend shortly before its second edition went to press.

Sharing our life and work with our children, Aneesha and Sachin, is the greatest pleasure we know. Their creativity and love nourish us every day. For more than a decade, our home in Madison has also been a perfect setting for writing and conversation about authors for whom we care deeply. This translation is dedicated to the memory of Vinay's father, Premanand Dharwadker, whose brilliance as an engineer left its mark on a few places in Asia: his time with us and our children was too short. The quotation in the dedication is from Vinay's poem 'The Civil Engineer', written in 1985 and published in *Sunday at the Lodi Gardens* (1994).

Madison, 15 August 2014   Aparna Dharwadker and
                                                Vinay Dharwadker

Introduction

APARNA DHARWADKER

Repositioning Mohan Rakesh and *Ashadh ka ek din*

Mohan Rakesh's *Ashadh ka ek din* is a foundational work of post-Independence urban Indian theatre, with a presence in the dual mediums of print and performance that has been continuous and influential since its first appearance in 1958. The play's revolutionary qualities in relation to the modern traditions of drama and theatre in India were immediately evident to its prescient readers and viewers. Among prominent scholar-critics, Nemichandra Jain described it as 'in a true sense the beginning of modern Hindi drama' because of its bold departure from earlier practices, and Namvar Singh observed that before Rakesh's arrival, 'one could not gauge the possibilities inherent in Hindi theatre. He proved for the first time that drama is an art worth taking seriously.'[1] The play also generated controversy because some vocal members of the Hindi literary establishment took exception to Rakesh's ambivalent portrayal of Kalidas, the classical Sanskrit poet-

1

playwright who had become an international symbol of Indian literary greatness in the course of the nineteenth century. The public criticism placed Rakesh on the defensive for a time, but he received the annual award for Best Play from the Sangeet Natak Akademi (the National Academy of Performing Arts) in 1959, and the Anamika group of Calcutta (now Kolkata) mounted the first major production of *Ashadh* the following year, under Shyamanand Jalan's direction. Over the next two decades, the play consolidated its position in the culture of contemporary urban performance through notable productions by nationally prominent directors, including Ebrahim Alkazi, Satyadev Dubey, Mohan Maharshi, Om Shivpuri, Amal Allana, and Rajinder Nath. *Ashadh ka ek din* was also translated into English, Bengali, Gujarati, Kannada, Marathi, Malayalam, Assamese, Manipuri, and Punjabi, but Hindi and English emerged as the most common languages of performance. This sustained attention from multiple points of view for more than fifty years has firmly established the play among the classics of contemporary drama and theatre, alongside such works as Dharamvir Bharati's *Andha yug* (Blind Epoch, Hindi, 1954), Badal Sircar's *Ebong indrajit* (And Indrajit, Bengali, 1962), Girish Karnad's *Tughlaq* (Kannada, 1964), and Vijay Tendulkar's *Shantata! Court chalu ahe* (Silence! The Court Is in Session, Marathi, 1967).

As a critical object, however, *Ashadh ka ek din* exemplifies an asymmetry that is more or less characteristic of every major work of modern Indian theatre. In a given play's original language of composition, and sometimes in other related languages, there are robust and extensive bodies of criticism, commentary, interpretation, and evaluation dealing with individual works, authors, movements, styles, and contexts. But in English, the primary link language that makes Indian-language plays available to national and international audiences, the 'function of criticism' in the quotidian cultural sphere has remained perfunctory and inadequate, especially within India. Even academic scholarship (located mainly in Western institutions) has only recently begun to make the kinds of substantive critical interventions that can establish modern Indian theatre studies as a serious field of study. As an author who is indubitably among the leading figures in twentieth-century Indian literature, regardless of language or genre, Mohan Rakesh is an especially egregious example of this epistemological gap. Since the early 1950s critics, writers, and scholars in Hindi have dealt with Rakesh as a fiction writer, playwright, theorist, essayist, literary editor, diarist, correspondent, and cultural observer on a scale that has created one of the most extensive and impressive critical traditions in modern Indian letters. In English, however, aside from reviews and other forms of commentary connected to specific performances, the body of criticism still consists of only a handful of interviews, journal articles, essays, and book chapters.[2]

The publication of this new authorized English translation of *Ashadh ka ek din*, in a format designed for worldwide circulation, is therefore a suitable occasion to place Rakesh and his work in the broader creative and critical contexts they deserve, and which are made possible by the medium of English. There are two critical perspectives that are especially pertinent to Rakesh and his drama, but have been only erratically associated with him so far. He is not only a 'modern' writer but a *postcolonial modernist* who defines a circumspect position for himself in relation to the effects of British colonialism, Euromodernism, and the complex literary history of a major modern Indian language such as Hindi, which in turn is embedded in the literary culture of the subcontinent at large. Correspondingly, *Ashadh ka ek din* is not only a revolutionary play in Hindi but a radical postcolonial intervention in the multiple Indian and European discourses that had developed during the nineteenth and early twentieth centuries around the authorial figure of Kalidas, classical Sanskrit literature, and the ostensible power of a past 'golden age' to shape a national literary and cultural renaissance in the present. The play accomplishes this, moreover, not through the conventional resources of the Western or Indian 'history play', but through scrupulous modernist innovation at the levels of text as well as performance, ranging from form, structure, language, characterization, and theme to mise en scène, visual affect, and stagecraft. *Ashadh ka ek din* is representative of Rakesh's oeuvre in all these respects—whatever their subject matter and setting, his plays, short stories, novels, and theoretical essays register a powerful rupture with the immediate (colonial) past, sometimes to connect omnitemporally with the remote past; and the scale of the representation in multiple genres makes him one of the leading Indian practitioners of what we now call 'geomodernism', in recognition of the cosmopolitan and planetary reach of modernism as a twentieth-century movement. Because of the singular position that Sanskrit literary culture and Kalidas occupy in modern conceptions of world literature, *Ashadh ka ek din* is, without exaggeration, a work without parallel in contemporary world theatre.

The play points to other important issues and relationships in need of further exploration. The first edition of June 1958 was followed by a second edition within three months, and both texts contained short prefaces that were virtual manifestos of modernist playwriting and emergent theatrical practices in post-Independence India. Rakesh commented briefly but suggestively on the state of modern theatre in Hindi, the relationship between Indian and Western theatre, the cultural functions of drama, and the playwright's role in the process of theatrical production. Historicizing the prefaces nearly six decades later reveals unexpected perspectives on modern Hindi and Indian theatre history, the idiosyncratic culture of playwriting and performance that existed around 1958, and the value Rakesh assigned to drama and theatre as cultural forms (see discussion in section 4 below; and Appendices 2 and 3).

The alternation between fiction and drama throughout his literary career, and the sometimes overt differences between these genres also suggest patterns of convergence and divergence in his body of work. During the 1950s, Rakesh had become closely associated with the *nai kahani* (new story) movement in Hindi, along with writers such as Kamleshwar, Rajendra Yadav, and Mannu Bhandari, and had published three collections of short stories, in 1950, 1957, and 1958. The appearance of *Ashadh ka ek din* in 1958, however, was not a sudden departure in a new direction in terms of genre and subject matter but a return to important earlier experiences. Rakesh had first encountered Sanskrit drama at the age of eleven, when he read Bhasa's *Pratima nataka* (Statue Play); later, as a student pursuing master's degrees in both Sanskrit and Hindi at Punjab University, Lahore (and subsequently

Jalandhar), in the mid-1940s and early 1950s, he immersed himself in classical Sanskrit literature and drama as well as the post-classical traditions of Hindi poetry, prose, and theatre. His experience of acting in Bhasa's *Svapna-vasavadatta* (The Dream of Vasavadatta) and of directing two other Sanskrit plays at the university first aroused his interest in translating a selection of the classic texts, but the difficulties he encountered in dealing with just the Induction to *Pratima nataka* led him to abandon the effort almost immediately. In 1949, Rakesh's investment in the drama form was confirmed by his first published work, a collection titled *Satya aur kalpana: chhah ekanki* (Truth and Imagination: Six One-Act Plays), and in 1956 he reportedly completed a play titled *Kalidas* which has not survived in manuscript. Written over a few weeks in early 1958 and published promptly, *Ashadh ka ek din* was therefore in part a sign that Rakesh's fascination with drama and the Sanskrit past had resurfaced in a different and decisive form: instead of *translating* Kalidas, the play *fictionalized* and *theatricalized* him, creating the infinitely complex and resonant relationships between classical Sanskrit and modern Hindi, history and fiction, reality and representation, and subject and object that are addressed in both this Introduction and the Afterword.

The juxtaposition of drama and prose fiction is, in fact, an intriguing and lifelong aspect of Rakesh's career. His three full-length plays—*Ashadh ka ek din*, *Laharon ke rajhans* (The Royal Swans of the Waves), and *Adhe adhure* (Half Formed, Half Unfinished)—appeared in 1958, 1963, and 1969, respectively, the first two dealing with seminal moments in antiquity and the third with the postcolonial urban present. After the experience of writing about Kalidas in his first full-length play, Rakesh returned to the challenge of translating Sanskrit drama, and published his versions of Shudraka's *Mrichchhakatika* (The Little Clay Cart) in 1961 and Kalidas's *Abhijnana-shakuntala* (titled *Shakuntal*) in 1965. His first novel, *Andhere band kamare* (Dark Sealed Rooms), also appeared in 1961, followed by *Na anevala kal* (The Tomorrow That Never Arrives) in 1968, and *Antaral* (Interval) in 1972. Collections of short stories were interspersed among these plays and novels, totalling five volumes and forty-six stories between 1950 and 1966, brought together in a four-volume edition between 1967 and 1969, with some additional stories chosen by Rakesh. Ten of these stories appeared again in a 1971 selection by Rakesh titled *Meri priya kahaniyan* (My Favourite Stories), and a second four-volume edition was issued between 1972 and 1974, the fourth book consisting of twelve uncollected stories compiled and edited by Kamleshwar. Other important works published during Rakesh's lifetime include a travelogue, *Akhiri chattan tak* (Up to the Last Rockface, 1953); a volume of reminiscences and belletristic pieces titled *Parivesh* (Frames of Reference, 1967); and three collections of writings by various hands edited by Rakesh, focusing, respectively, on literary self-portraits (1965), creative non-fiction about cities (1965), and one-act plays (1970). The remainder of Rakesh's corpus consists of a succession of posthumously published collections, which include one-act plays, radio plays, letters, diaries, theatre essays and criticism, cultural criticism, and uncollected writings in various genres (see the Chronology for a complete listing).

If drama and prose fiction, then, are the two principal genres with which Rakesh engaged during his own lifetime, the similarities and differences between them as modernist mediums, and his specific self-interrogations as a playwright, are dimensions of his creative life that deserve fuller discussion. Furthermore, *Ashadh ka ek din* has to be connected to, and read in conjunction with, the theoretical positions on drama and theatre at which Rakesh hinted in the two prefaces to the play, and which he developed in his criticism during the 1960s. The following sections of this Introduction deal sequentially with these critical issues, introducing new literary-performative contexts for the text of the play, but also bringing to readers in English relevant material from a range of Hindi sources authored by Rakesh, his fellow artists, and his critics.

Ashadh ka ek din and Postcolonial Modernism

In *Theatres of Independence*, I argued that for Rakesh's purposes in *Ashadh*,

> far more important than the historicity of Kalidas's life or work . . . is his iconic role in the colonial and postcolonial constructions of Indian literature, culture, civilization, and nationhood, well-known to Rakesh as a trained reader of Sanskrit, a modern Hindi author, and a postcolonial literary modernist. In theatricalizing Kalidas, therefore, Rakesh takes on a body of commentary, exegesis, scholarship, criticism, and ideological mythmaking that spans nearly two millennia, and encompasses the Indian literary and cultural past from classical to postcolonial times.[3]

The important strains in this network of discourses are Indian as well as European.[4] From the seventh century onward, Kalidas served as an arch-canonical figure in Indian traditions of poetry, poetics, drama, and critical commentary, and as the touchstone for both the major forms of classical composition—*natya* (drama) and *kavya* (poetry). In 1789, Sir William Jones's translation of *Shakuntala*, and the preface in which he announced his discovery of Sanskrit to European readers, initiated the orientalist philological tradition that proclaimed Sanskrit as the premier Indian language, drama as its most highly evolved form, and Kalidas as its foremost practitioner. Eagerly embracing this Anglo-European revaluation of Indian antiquity, late-colonial Indian nationalists appropriated Kalidas as the symbol of a redeeming ancient civilization, and placed him at the centre of a national literary and cultural renaissance. In a parallel modern trajectory, major European figures, including Johann Wolfgang von Goethe, Friedrich Schiller, Edward Gordon Craig, Jerzy Grotowski, and Eugenio Barba, singled out *Shakuntala* as the exemplary work of 'Indian drama' and created a reception history for it that is more complex than that of any other Indian text.[5] Finally, in cultural-nationalist discourses of the post-Independence period, Kalidas has continued to symbolize the fabled past with which a decolonizing culture should reconnect, and he now serves as one of the exemplars for a new, 'authentically Indian' theatre.

In *Ashadh ka ek din*, Rakesh deliberately disrupts these cross-cultural hagiographies of Kalidas and bases his modernist reimagining of the past on a systematic violation of expectations. In place of the legendary *mahakavi* (great poet) of Indian tradition, he creates a sensitive and troubled but self-centred aesthete who is unable to resolve the competing claims of creativity, ambition, and love. This self-absorbed private self appears in the foreground; the epic oeuvre that is the basis of Kalidas's extraordinary fame becomes a seemingly effortless offstage production tangential to his social, romantic, and spiritual crises. Similarly, instead of the self-possessed metropolitan poet vital to the narrative of Indian 'classicism', Rakesh portrays a provincial prodigy who departs reluctantly from the poetic landscape of his origin, remains alienated from the world of fame and power in the imperial city, and returns to his village at the end to reconnect (unsuccessfully) with his past life. To the extent that the play deals with the classical author's work, poetry clearly overshadows drama: the conversation between Nikshep and Mallika at the beginning of Act Two makes a passing reference to the plays Kalidas has written for the 'entertainment halls' in Ujjayini, and Kalidas himself refers to *Shakuntala* only once in his long monologue in Act Three. As the Afterword demonstrates, the relationship between Rakesh's play and the classical authorial figure of Kalidas is irreducibly complex, but Rakesh-the-playwright does noticeably evade an *overt* confrontation with his most daunting precursor in the tradition of 'Indian theatre'. The modalities of *Ashadh* are also broadly antithetical to those of Kalidas's poetry and drama—while the latter emphasize the heroic and erotic modes (*vira rasa* and *shringara rasa*), Rakesh resorts to irony and tragedy. Instead of the happy resolutions of Kalidas's plays and the exquisite refinement of his poetry, we witness the unhappy drama *of* Kalidas—a displaced Dushyanta for whom there is no ring of recollection, and no reunion with the beloved. The dialogue of the play also 'contaminates' the classical with the vernacular as it combines a formal Sanskritized vocabulary appropriate to the historical setting with mid-twentieth-century 'conversational' Hindi syntax and diction, producing a synthesis that registers the polarities of culture at the level of language without appearing either artificial or forced.

All these features of *Ashadh* seem to be more or less consistent with those of the modern history play, but in at least three respects Rakesh's radical practice goes further. Kalidas is the *only* historical figure in his representation: all the others are fictional inventions who play designated roles in a parable-like narrative about art and the artist. Instead of the large cast of characters and grand temporal sweep evident even in modern Anglo-American history plays like Bernard Shaw's *Saint Joan* and Arthur Miller's *The Crucible*, Rakesh's play contains only four principal characters and a single, spare village setting. Further, Kalidas may be the protagonist but he is not the central character in his own story—that role belongs to Mallika, the fictional lover and muse who both actively and reactively constructs her life around the choices Kalidas makes, and descends into poverty, prostitution, and illegitimate motherhood as he ascends the political-cultural ladder. Rather than evoking any known account of the poet's life, these patterns of sympathy and antipathy develop the thematically significant binaries of man/woman, love/ambition, success/failure, and centre/periphery, problematizing the specific history of Kalidas as well as the form of the history play.

This powerful modernist swerve away from convention and tradition in *Ashadh ka ek din* is made possible by creative and critical principles that emerge from Rakesh's historical self-positioning, and inform his work as a whole. He regards the event of Partition in 1947 as the beginning of a crisis that enveloped the generation of writers who came to maturity in the 1954–64 period, giving this decade the same transformative role that the 1910s performed in Anglo-modernism. The key theoretical terms for the work produced by this generation are *nai* or *naya* (new) and *adhunik* ('modern', but also 'modernist'), both terms designating not radically unfamiliar areas of human experience (which Rakesh claims is an existential impossibility) but clear differences of outlook (*drishtikon*), feeling and sensation (*samvedana*), and consciousness (*chetana*). In Rakesh's case, the commitment to newness entails a sense of historical distance from seminal late-colonial figures in Hindi, such as Bharatendu Harishchandra, and a more urgent sense of absolute and irreconcilable difference from his immediate precursors, who include authors such as Jai Shankar Prasad, Mahadevi Varma, and Ramdhari Singh Dinkar. In an essay appropriately titled *'Imaraten tutane par'* ('On the Collapse of Structures'), he argues:

> In the clash between an emerging consciousness and a collapsing traditionalism, any talk of a compromise, of 'taking the good and rejecting the bad in both', seems pointless and unfounded. This is not a crisis of relative achievements, about what is good in one or the other, but of two radically opposite visions that cannot be reconciled under any circumstances.[6]

The iconoclastic vision, moreover, is sustained by the principle of artistic autonomy, which gives a writer the freedom to follow his or her own aesthetic and ideological goals, regardless of the 'offence' to more traditional sensibilities.

Approached in this way, the 'new' Kalidas of *Ashadh ka ek din* is not only a displacement of the iconic figure of orientalist and cultural-nationalist tradition—he also provides Rakesh with an occasion for rethinking the idea of 'greatness' in history, redefining the genre of the history play, and bringing the remote past meaningfully into the mid-twentieth-century present. Rakesh's substantive statements on these questions appear in the preface to the first edition of his second full-length play, *Laharon ke rajhans* (1963), in which he acknowledges that 'many kinds of arguments arose in relation to the first play [*Ashadh*], regarding its historical accuracy, its theatrical possibilities and, most of all, its portrayal of the character of Kalidas'. On the issue of fidelity to history, he argues that there are no indisputable 'facts' about Kalidas's life, only conjectures that have hardened into orthodoxy to support particular ideological-cultural agendas and 'ingrained prejudices'. Hence, Rakesh regards the resistance to his demystification of Kalidas not as a contest over the 'facts' of history but as the symptom of an uncritical, adulatory traditionalism which 'always want[s] to place our civilizational symbols on a superhuman plane. . . . The principal reason for this may be that we have no trust in our own humanity, no faith in our own reality. Since we expect nothing from ourselves, it seems impossible to us that one can remain on a human level and still accomplish something great. That greatness is possible *only* at a human level—this would probably be too hard for us even to contemplate.'[7] In Rakesh's view, his portrait of Kalidas is consonant with the authorial self implied in works such as

Abhijnana-shakuntala, *Kumara-sambhava*, and *Meghaduta*, and has greater psychological credibility than the idealized figure of popular lore and cultural-nationalist discourse. Moreover, the Kalidas of *Ashadh* is not 'weak' but 'vulnerable, unstable, and harrowed by his inner struggles'; his alter ego Vilom appears stronger only because he has put an end to such turmoil: 'In *Ashadh ka ek din*, the defeated man is not the despairing Kalidas, but the self-possessed Vilom.'[8]

Rakesh's second important move in this preface is to draw on the experience of writing two plays with historical protagonists—*Ashadh* in 1958 and *Laharon ke rajhans* by 1963—in order to theorize the relation of history to historical fictions. 'Dependence on history or historical figures,' he argues, 'does not turn literature into history. . . . [H]istory is not expressed in literature through its incontrovertible events, but through an imagination that links events together and creates a distinct, new history of its own kind. This creation is not history in the conventional sense. To look for that kind of history one really should go to the scholarly tomes of historians.'[9] The connection of history to the present is also not literal or analogical but symbolic: Kalidas is not so much an individual as a representation of the 'creative energies' within Indian culture, and of the internal struggles that destabilize the 'artistic imagination' in every age. Rakesh chose the specific figure of Kalidas for this symbolism because he felt that he 'could not find a better label, a better signifier for our cumulative creative energies'.[10] Besides, it was 'very convenient to exploit a deep-rooted sentiment. . . . With the name Kalidas, *which is an accepted thing with the people*, I did not have to create an image' (emphasis added).[11] Instead of expending his energies on the invention of a character 'about whose dilemma or mental struggle people would not be convinced', he decided to 'take a symbol from history and use my energies in creating a play for and of today'.[12]

The play speaks in and for the present because 'contemporariness' inheres not in any particular subject matter but in the author's consciousness. Rakesh is especially outspoken on this issue because of the conspicuous difference between his own fiction and drama: his stories and novels are set uniformly in the postcolonial urban and semi-urban present, whereas two of his three full-length plays deal with remote antiquity. Consequently, he asserts that a historical setting does not preclude relevance in the present, and a present-day setting is not in itself a sign of modernity. In an essay in English titled 'Looking Around as a Playwright' (1966), Rakesh defines contemporariness as

> a phenomenon of the mind that gives a particular direction to its faculties and makes it see and interpret things in a light that emerges from the events and attributes of the age. It is not the things and events here and now that are contemporary, but the way in which one sees them. . . . No work of art is ever modern because of its subject; if it is modern, it is so because of the way in which that subject has been treated.[13]

Notwithstanding the historical protagonists of his first two plays and his two translations from classical Sanskrit drama, Rakesh declares that he is 'not really aware of having written anything that is not contemporary'.[14]

We can, then, adapt two classic modernist formulations in T.S. Eliot's essay 'Tradition and the Individual Talent' (1919) to place this important form of geomodernism in perspective. Rakesh's generation created 'new, really new' works of art, many of which showed an awareness 'not only of the pastness of the past, but of its presence; . . . a sense of the timeless as well as of the temporal and of the timeless and the temporal together'. Eliot describes this awareness as the effect of a 'historical sense' which 'makes a writer traditional. And it is at the same time what makes the writer acutely conscious of his place in time, of his own contemporaneity.'[15] But in Rakesh's postcolonial practice, the historical sense and the writer's consciousness of his place in time function differently: his plays connect him to the present by questioning and destabilizing the traditions of a supposedly perfect past, while his novels and stories immerse themselves fully in an imperfect present.

Gender, Patronage, and the Politics of Language

The anti-traditionalism of *Ashadh ka ek din*, stressed by the author, his audience, and his interpreters in the theatre, is the ultimate justification for the liberties Rakesh takes with the past. But its modernity (and contemporaneity) also emerges in several other thematic emphases to which history is peripheral. In the figures of Mallika and Ambika, the play creates a new kind of female subject, as challenging to conventional Indian notions of femininity as the character of Kalidas is to literary and cultural tradition. Mallika is the transhistorical muse whose beauty, sympathy, and loyalty are claimed to an extraordinary extent by the extraordinarily gifted poet. In rejecting convention, respectability, and the possibility of happiness in her own life, Mallika is the first mature heroine in modern Indian theatre to disrupt the equation of idealized Indian femininity with marriage, domesticity, chastity, and legitimate motherhood. Her opposition to marriage is not an empty gesture: already in Act One of the play, she knows the price of her defiance, yet she persists because for her the bond of feeling has a purity and permanence that places it above all other relations. She also asserts an essentially modern sense of selfhood: 'Mallika's life is her own property. If she wants to destroy it, then who has the right to criticize her?' (see p. 90). This claim to self-possession—a modernist rupture— is radical in a patriarchal culture that empowers women in mythic, religious, and political contexts but is compelled to silence them in the sexual and domestic roles of lover, wife, and mother.

Similarly, Ambika deviates strongly from the Indian cultural stereotypes of unquestioning maternal love and passive female suffering, emerging instead as a woman embittered but not vanquished by a life of struggle and disappointment. She rejects the Kalidas–Mallika relationship not merely, or even especially, because it defies convention, but because she sees it as driven entirely by the poet's selfish needs and lacking in mutuality. When Kalidas expresses indifference towards public recognition, Ambika dismisses his 'doubts' as self-important posturing. When Mallika refuses to impede the poet's progress by bringing up the question of marriage, Ambika counters that Kalidas has no intention of doing so himself:

I understand his kind of man very well. His only connection with you is that you're a receptacle and a refuge through which he can love himself, be proud of himself. But aren't you a flesh-and-blood person? Don't you—and doesn't he—have any obligation towards you?
[see p. 101]

When the courtly visitors invade her home (in Act Two), Ambika knows that Kalidas is trying to assuage his guilt, but will not have the courage to face Mallika. Hence her fury at the intrusion, her attempts to denounce Kalidas before his royal wife, and her judgement that he is not worthy of Mallika's grief. She directs her critique at the self-centred, outwardly ascetic, creative male self, which is no less destructive of Mallika's innocence and happiness than Vilom's sexual predations.

The unconventionality of the two main female characters has not, however, prevented the perception that Rakesh's iconoclasm in *Ashadh ka ek din* is compromised by a rather conventional masculinist insistence on feminine endurance. Mallika resists patriarchy in one respect, but capitulates to it in another, because the fulfilment of male creative promise is the ideal to which she willingly sacrifices her life. Despite her passion for beauty, creativity, and deep feeling, Mallika is ultimately a passive figure who finds vicarious fulfilment in someone else's ambition, and even after years of suffering, offers no reproach. Not surprisingly, each of the play's three acts ends with an act of abandonment on the part of Kalidas: when he leaves for Ujjayini alone (Act One); when he deliberately avoids a meeting with Mallika during his subsequent visit to the village (Act Two); and when he leaves her home abruptly at the end, unable to endure the shape of her present life (Act Three). For all his ambivalence towards Kalidas, Rakesh also clearly romanticizes Mallika's self-negation. In the preface to *Laharon ke rajhans*, he comments that Kalidas and Vilom 'are not in themselves the signifiers of victory and defeat—that signifier is Mallika, who is the fully articulated form of Kalidas's faith. Mallika's character is not only that of lover and muse, but also of that rooted, unwavering constancy which is not destroyed at its source even though it withers on the surface.'[16] That Mallika retains her autonomy in relation to everyone except Kalidas, and Kalidas admits at the end that she has been the only subject of his poetry, implies a vision of creativity in which a woman's suffering is the necessary price of a man's achievement. Ambika's critique attacks this presumption but cannot dislodge it, because her rage prevents neither the destruction of Mallika's life nor her own abject end.

If Mallika and Ambika are ambivalent portraits of the 'new Indian woman', the overtly socio-literary thematic in the play is concerned with the relation of art to state patronage and of the centre to the periphery—both vital issues in a new nation where literary and theatrical 'art' (unlike mass cultural forms like film and television) could not be economically self-sustaining, and a 'national' literature could not, in important respects, be more than an aggregation of 'regional' literatures. The persistent legend of Kalidas—textualized in a seventeenth-century Tibetan-Buddhist source—is that of a country fool who was thrust into courtly life through subterfuge, but transformed himself into a supreme poet through determination and the grace of his patron-goddess Kali (hence the name 'Kalidas', the 'servant of Kali').[17] Rakesh recasts the legend as the story of the self-conscious genius from the provinces who conquers the metropolis through sheer talent, renounces his success because of his nostalgia for an uncorrupted life, and finds at the end that he is a stranger in both environments. While this narrative seems to uphold the anti-romantic modernist view of the artist, *Ashadh* is also the first self-reflexive text to address issues pertinent to post-Independence Indian forms of authorship in both literature and theatre: the privileges and obligations of patronage, the poet's relationship with his audience, the effects of public recognition, and the unequal relation of village to city.

In the preface to the second edition of the play, Rakesh asserts that the writer's relation to state patronage is the most important 'sign of contemporaneity' in the work, without which the wrenching irony of Kalidas and Mallika's lives would not have emerged clearly. 'In this play,' he comments in a later interview with Carlo Coppola, 'I wanted to portray the dilemma of the present-day writer, a writer lured by the sort of temptations being offered by the state . . . and his commitment to himself. . . . The play is about the contemporary mind'.[18] In line with this view, noted director Satyadev Dubey presented Kalidas in his 1964 production as 'the embodiment of the modern artist, obsessed with his creative problems but [smarting] under the humiliations heaped by the establishment', while in his 1972 production Faisal Alkazi attempted to stress the 'general applicability' of the play's central problem—'how a creative artist is completely crushed and broken by a system'.[19] The imperial court in *Ashadh*, described but never shown directly on stage, is certainly a plausible analogue for a postcolonial nation state in which a centralized cultural bureaucracy (embodied in the Sahitya Akademi, the Lalit Kala Akademi, and the Sangeet Natak Akademi) plays a decisive role in fostering cultural forms, the institution of theatre is organized along patronal rather than commercial lines, and the state's support has economic as well as symbolic value. In Rakesh's opinion, Indian writers handle the consequent struggle—between the writer's need for survival and recognition and the principle of artistic autonomy—with singular ineptitude: 'If they were really indifferent to money or to the returns on their writing, then many of them wouldn't be seen seeking those favors which would compromise their egos, their conscience, and everything of this sort.'[20] In the play, Kalidas is afraid that to accept a court sinecure is to prostitute his talent, but as his 'neutral' friend Nikshep reminds everyone,

> Opportunity doesn't wait for anybody. If Kalidas doesn't leave this place, the court won't lose anything. The office of court poet won't remain vacant. But, for the rest of his life, Kalidas will remain what he is today—a local poet! Even the people who're praising *A Gathering of Seasons* today will forget him in a short while. [see p. 109]

This is the essential quandary—the state recognizes and rewards talent on its own terms, but the artist who does not seize the opportunity for recognition risks oblivion. Kalidas's ambivalence resonates in Rakesh's diary entry for 6 February 1959, where he expresses irritation at the 'scandal' caused by his representation of Kalidas, along with a realistic sense of what is at stake:

> I've already accepted that somebody else will receive the Sangeet Natak Akademi prize—although Awasthi [Suresh Awasthi, Secretary of the Akademi] did say the other day, 'Friend, the rumour is that your play's getting the prize. It's very high up.' I don't know. Nor do I want to know. One unnecessarily ruins one's sleep. I feel vexed only on account of the publishers, otherwise except for living on the royalties from my books, I don't want to anticipate or expect anything. But how can this be done? How? One publisher has sent twenty-four rupees as my six-month earnings, while another has sent eight rupees as the outstanding balance for a whole year! Heavens![21]

However, after Rakesh had won the Akademi award and strengthened his reputation as a literary playwright, a radio broadcast of the play in October 1959 caused an equal and opposite reaction against the state's appropriation of his work: 'Last night they broadcast AKED [*Ashadh*] as a national play. I felt like committing suicide after listening to it. And I feel like destroying all that I have written.'[22] Of course, Kalidas's crisis (unlike Rakesh's) is not that the imperial court trivializes his work, but that poetry becomes merely a stage in his advancement to full-fledged political life under a new name, and proves to be a liability.

The poet's disaffection, then, brings the court to his village and the centre–periphery dichotomy into the foreground, along with its distinctive implications for an old-but-new, traditional-but-modern, multilingual-but-hierarchical postcolonial culture. In *Ashadh* the imperial metropolis is the converse of the village, and can regard the latter only in three ways—as an idyllic retreat from the depredations of politics, as an exotic source of poetic inspiration, and as a second-rate cultural space. These perceptions are at a significant remove from the city–village opposition that informs two influential but antithetical visions of the modern Indian nation—Mahatma Gandhi's idea of the village as the critical socio-economic and political unit in independent India and Nehru's commitment to modernization, urbanization, and industrial development. Rakesh does not address the issue of political economy directly; instead, he depicts the village as a stimulus for literary experiences that the city cannot comprehend, but which it romanticizes and celebrates with empty bureaucratic gestures. Far worse than Princess Priyangumanjari's unconscious cruelty in this respect is the encounter (in Act Two) of rural simplicity with urban bureaucratic protocol, the epitome of mediocrity and sterility. In the play's most darkly comic moments, Anusvar and Anunasik—interchangeable male courtiers whose names derive satirically from nasal sounds or 'vowel nasality' in the Devanagari alphabet—parody bureaucratic inaction by finding every possible self-important reason not to perform their assigned task (of preparing Mallika's home for the princess's arrival). Needless to say, such a tableau has enormous resonance in a context where artists are contemptuous of the nation state's cultural bureaucracy in the same measure that they are subject to its whims. More ironically, Rakesh as the arch-metropolitan, cosmopolitan, modernist author seems to turn the tables on his own craft by portraying the village as the realm of beauty and inspiration, and the city as sterile, silly, intellectually second-rate.

The final arena of centre–periphery interactions is language. The female aesthetes in the play, Rangini and Sangini, are disappointed to find that Mallika speaks much the same language as them, and there are no 'local' terms for everyday objects and spaces in the village. They want to engage Mallika in learned debate about dialectal differences in Sanskrit, and when Mallika resists their literalism about Kalidas's metaphors, they take offence and accuse her of doubting the truth of his poetry. This imperialism of Sanskrit in Rakesh's play has contemporary analogues in three kinds of hierarchical relations: those within a major Indian literary language like Hindi, between a dominant form and several subordinate dialects; those among the various Indian languages, where one language may dominate several others; and those between Indian languages and the language of modern-day imperialism, English. Rakesh describes English as a 'comfortable coat' which might make him look smart, but does not suit the contours of his body. At the same time, through the pedantry of the courtiers in *Ashadh* he mocks the artificially elevated Hindi of the 'Hindi enthusiasts', which is 'no language at all [but] only a set of phrases and certain haphazard things put together, a particular type of vocabulary which, quite frankly, mean nothing to me. . . . It's the kind of Hindi which is not the mature language, literarily speaking; it's the language of state patronage.'[23]

However, just as there are dominant and subordinate traditions within each Indian language, and some Indian languages are dominant over others, *all* indigenous languages occupy increasingly marginal positions in relation to English, which today must be recognized as an Indian as much as a Western language. Indeed, at the beginning of the twenty-first century, the subordination of the village is an equally plausible metaphor for the relative insignificance of the stay-at-home in comparison with the diasporic writer, who travels, Kalidas-like, to metropolitan centres completely outside his or her culture of origin. In the last three decades, the singular success of Indian English writers (especially novelists) in the West has transformed the contemporary understanding of 'Indian' writing, and initiated a new politics of language in postcolonial literary production. For instance, in the introduction to *Mirrorwork* (1997), an anthology of '50 years of Indian writing', Salman Rushdie claims that 'the prose writing—both fiction and non-fiction—created in this period by Indian writers working in English, is proving to be a stronger and more important body of work than most of what has been produced in the 16 "official languages" of India, the so-called "vernacular languages", during the same time'.[24] Coming from a writer whose family belongs to the privileged 'upper crust' of Indian and Pakistani society, and who left India at the age of thirteen (in 1960) for a boarding-school education in England, this statement captures precisely the metropolitan arrogance that has invested the characters of Rangini and Sangini, Anusvar and Anunasik, in *Ashadh* with a prescient irony.

The sociocultural meanings that the play has thus accumulated since its appearance in 1958 suggest an interesting correlation: if, for Rakesh, Kalidas is more important as a symbolic rather than a historical figure, the *symbolic reduction* of this historical figure is ideologically more significant than the literal details of the drama. For the play to carry the powerful anti-traditionalist, anti-hagiographic message that directors, performers, theatre audiences, and readers have celebrated, it is sufficient that Rakesh adopts an ironic rather than heroic or romantic attitude towards his subject. By refusing to create an idealized author as the creator of an ideal poetic oeuvre, Rakesh follows in part the modernist dictum of separating the poet from his work; by placing the poet in deterministic institutional contexts, he inserts postcolonial perspectives into modernist formations. His emphasis on the fallibility of cultural heroes, moreover, applies to modern political and literary icons like Gandhi, Nehru, and Rabindranath Tagore as much as to the ancient figure of Kalidas. With these objectives, Rakesh is able to circumvent both an analogical and allegorical relation to history, and to showcase his parabolic narrative about poetry and the poet. Even within the tradition of post-Independence historical drama that it initiates, *Ashadh ka ek din* stands apart due to its economy and starkness, and its insistence that historical 'accuracy' and 'authenticity' are tangential to a subject that belongs to the realm of cultural mythmaking.

Rakesh, 'Drama', and 'Theatre'

In the opening sentence of this Introduction, I referred to the continuous and influential presence that *Ashadh ka ek din* has maintained in the dual realms of print and performance since its first appearance. Rakesh belongs, in fact, to the first generation of playwrights in modern Indian theatre who achieved this balance fully, and contributed in equal measure to 'drama' (the aggregation of texts) and 'theatre' (institutionalized performance). He was more consistently interested than other early post-Independence playwrights, however, in defining his goals in relation to both activities, creating integral connections between them, and situating them in relation to past practices and future possibilities. The inaugural statements of these lifelong concerns are the short prefaces to the two editions of *Ashadh* that appeared in 1958.

The first preface deserves to be quoted in full because of the startling brevity with which it delinks the contemporary Hindi stage from both colonial-Indian and Western theatre, and announces the beginning of a postcolonial-modernist turn in urban theatre that is equally mindful of drama as text and as performance.

Drama in Hindi has no links with any particular theatrical tradition. All we have before us are the accomplishments of Western theatre. But the conditions of our life do not ask for those accomplishments, nor does it seem possible for us to consecrate that theatrecraft amongst us on a large scale without any changes.

The idea of the development of the Hindi stage certainly does not imply that government or semi-governmental institutions should come up with performance spaces equipped with ultramodern facilities here and there so that Hindi plays may be presented in them. The question is not merely one of financial convenience but also of a certain cultural vision. The Hindi stage will have to take a leading role in representing the cultural achievements and aspirations of the Hindi-speaking region, in expressing the richness and variety of our aesthetic sensibilities. The kind of stage that is needed to present the colourful texture of our daily life, to express our sensations and pulsations, will be quite different from the Western stage. The constitutive features of this stage will come to life with the help of theatrical experimentation, and it will continue its development in the hands of capable actors and directors.

It is possible that this play may contribute something towards the search for those possibilities.[25]

Virtually every sentence in this text takes up a radical position or puts forward a radical proposition. First, Rakesh's primary concern with Hindi rather than 'Indian' theatre is symptomatic of the ways in which region connects with nation in the densely layered map of India's multilingual literacy. As a major modern Indian language, Hindi is at one level a self-sufficient medium with its own continuous literary history; but as the country's majority language, and as one of the two official link languages (along with English), it also has a national presence and significance as a creative instrument. What Rakesh says about 'drama in Hindi' and the 'Hindi stage' thus applies, with appropriate qualifications, to drama and theatre in India.

Second, Rakesh's opening claim, that drama in Hindi 'has no links with any particular theatrical tradition', dismisses at one stroke the entire colonial legacy of urban commercial theatre. The overlapping mediums of Hindi, Hindustani, and Urdu had dominated the Bombay-based Parsi theatre of the late-colonial period that was described as India's first 'national theatre', but as Rakesh comments in '*Hindi rangmanch*' ('The Hindi Stage'), it was a ridiculous spectacle modelled on second-rate Western theatre, and could create only a 'low and rotten' legacy for theatre in Hindi.[26] He therefore does not accept its performance texts as constituting 'drama in Hindi', nor does he recognize the Parsi enterprise as representing a usable 'theatrical tradition'. Like the left-wing activists of the Indian People's Theatre Association in the 1940s, and the bourgeois-nationalist scholars and critics who promoted state patronage of the arts after Independence in 1947, Rakesh-as-modernist also rejects the colonial model of theatre as commercialized entertainment. But, as his critique of major colonial-era precursors in Hindi makes clear, the obverse of commerce is not literary drama divorced from performance, or the unperformable closet play. Bharatendu Harishchandra, for example, was a late-nineteenth-century pioneer in drama who failed in the theatre due to limited means and the absence of support, while in the early twentieth century Jai Shankar Prasad 'broke away from the Parsi company traditions, but neither advanced Bharatendu's tradition nor created any sign of a new tradition in theatre'.[27] Both literary icons separated 'drama as verbal text' from 'theatre as popular performance', but the effect, especially of Prasad's refined language, thematic gravity, and literary perfection, was such that 'the very consciousness of the relationship between drama and the stage disappeared' from the playwright's craft.[28] Rakesh's explicit goal, stated in the first preface to *Ashadh*, is to restore this relationship without artistic compromises.

Third, Rakesh categorically rejects Western theatre as a

model for Hindi or Indian playwrights, because the form, structure, technique, and content of that theatre are all equally alienated from, and incompatible with, his primary subject—ordinary life and everyday experience in India. In comparison with print genres such as fiction and poetry, a performative genre like theatre must be especially careful to avoid replicating the modes of developed nations, because such imitations create a false sense of avant-gardism without accomplishing anything real. The Hindi stage, as Rakesh notes, has to represent the 'cultural achievements and aspirations' of its immediate audience, and in a later essay, *'Natak-kar aur rangmanch'* ('The Playwright and the Stage'), he explains how this mission separates him from the 'mimic men' of his generation:

> [Their] vision is concerned with giving the stage a 'new' and 'modern' look from the outside, and not with searching for a theatre within our personal lives and circumstances. For that quest we need a deep understanding of our life and environment—a clear recognition of the theatrical possibilities of the assaults and counter-assaults on our sensibilities. Only this quest can lead us in the direction of really new experiments, and give shape to that theatrecraft with which even we have not yet become acquainted.[29]

Elsewhere, Rakesh mocks those for whom 'real life can only be lived outside this country, new literary experiments are possible only in other languages, the problems of the age are born only in the Atlantic and Pacific continents, and the true touch of modernity can be felt only in the air of Europe and America'.[30] His particular kind of modernity demands that Indian-language theatre first give adequate expression to the existence around it, to its 'lived world', or *Lebenswelt*, and only then approach the national and the global.

Finally, Rakesh proposes a performance culture mediated not by state patronage but by voluntary, energetic, and creative collaboration among all those committed to theatre. In other words, the rejection of commercialized theatre is not an invitation to the state to step in as primary impresario of theatre activity in the nation. Rakesh's specifically theatrical expectations for *Ashadh ka ek din* and the need to bring plays quickly on to the stage are the main concerns of his preface to the second edition of the play, which appeared in September 1958. It is clear from this document that Rakesh is disconcerted by the absence of a major stage production of *Ashadh* not only before but after publication, because he believes firmly in an integral connection between drama's two modes of existence, and hence between playwriting and the production process.

> I believe that the real value of a dramatic work—its success or failure—is decided only on the stage. If good, successful plays are to be written, it really would be appropriate to expect that they be performed on stage before publication, and be given their final textual form only in light of that experience. But I think it will take us some years to get to such a phase.[31]

As it happened, Rakesh's keen interest in engaging with the production of his work, and in using the 'theatre' to modify his 'drama', was realized a few years later, when Anamika's 1966 production of *Laharon ke rajhans* in Calcutta led to his sustained collaboration with Shyamanand Jalan. Rakesh's long and eclectic preface to the third edition of this play (1968), which consists of commentary, recollections, diary entries, and letters, records in detail the intensive year-long period (August 1965–July 1966) during which Jalan, who was the play's director *and* lead actor, became both sceptical interlocutor and sympathetic facilitator for Rakesh, contributing to a thorough revision of the final act.[32] With the actors also testing out the dialogue and narrative arc throughout the rehearsal process, the performance script reached its final form only two days before the opening show. In 'The Playwright and the Stage', probably written in 1967, Rakesh recalls the entire experience as an optimal and even unprecedented realization of the text–performance relation:

> At least in the context of Hindi drama, this was perhaps the first time that the processes of writing and presentation could be joined together in this manner. I think that the congenial atmosphere I found in Calcutta to make this possible is the only kind in which a real search for theatre can be carried out—both at the level of writing and at the level of directing.[33]

The two prefaces to *Ashadh* in 1958 thus argue for the reinvention of both drama and theatre in urban India, and anticipate the positioning of the playwright-artist at the centre of both activities. Because this interdependence has lifelong significance for Rakesh's career as a playwright, it is important to recognize the balance of power he creates between the two modes. Drama for Rakesh is a word-centred form susceptible to the same writerly struggles with language and structure as other literary genres (such as prose fiction and poetry), but not interchangeable with them because of its unique expressive potential. The essay 'Looking Around as a Playwright' sets up this perspective by describing the act of playwriting as the expression of an irrepressible urge and a psychic struggle that cannot be fulfilled through other forms:

> What concerns me most is my desire to write, or to put it more aptly, my inability to help writing plays. The forces inside and outside me create a sort of compulsion . . . to express and communicate something that is by its own nature dramatic. . . . I find myself under the sway of this 'something' happening—to me as well as around me; something that is a force, a conflict and a terrible irony. At every step it strikes me down, but again lifts me to my feet—by that contradicting and negating itself. What is this great 'something'? I do not know. It is in the air, in the age, in me. I know it is there, but cannot give it a name. May be I want to write drama only because I cannot give it a name.[34]

This almost rhapsodic view of playwriting is also inseparable from Rakesh's firm, even stubborn, insistence on the instrumental role of language in drama and theatre, especially in the post-cinema age. A remarkable proportion of Rakesh's discussions of theatre focus on 'the word', appearing in essays with titles such as 'Words and the Stage', 'Word and

Resonance', 'The Changing Role of Words in Theatre', and, most of all, in his project for the prestigious two-year Nehru Fellowship, titled 'The Dramatic Word'. In a conversation with the Russian writer Aleksei Arbuzov (*'Rangmanch aur shabda'* ['Theatre and the Word']), he argues that drama and theatre have to be regarded as primarily verbal–aural rather than visual forms because, in mimetic terms, aurality is what separates film from drama: 'the fundamental difference between the two mediums is that in one, the visual expectation gives birth to the word, and in the other, the verbal expectation gives birth to the scene'.[35] As emphasized by the classical Indian theory of theatre as *drishya kavya* (visual poetry, poetry presented as spectacle), words and images are certainly interdependent in both media, but for Rakesh the word is central to drama, and the image to film; in theatre, the visual serves as the *embodiment* of the word, rather than as an end in itself .

Rakesh clarifies that word-centredness in theatre does not imply an untheatrical or anti-theatrical 'literariness'— words have to achieve not literary effects but the resonances appropriate to a particular dramatic structure. The importance of 'writing' also leads him to question the claim that theatre, like film, is a 'director's medium': for him the dramatic text exists apart from the staging process, and regarding the director as the sole orchestrator of the performance event is to create an artistic void in theatre. The ideal that Rakesh posits in theory and practice is of an equal collaboration between living author, director, and performers, but there is no discursive context in which he is willing to cede the priority of the playwright as author, and of drama as text. To the 'objection' that his thinking is determined by drama and not other, less text-centred forms of theatre, his rejoinder is that 'my prime concern is this form of theatre only'.[36]

The most important attribute of the theatre corresponding to this conception of drama is its freedom from technological artifice. Rakesh considers the obsession with technical accomplishments irrelevant to real theatre, though his objection is not to technology per se but an overdependence on it. Reiterating his resistance to capitalist intrusions in theatre, he argues in 'Theatre without Walls' that it is time to

> extricate theatre from its dependence on 'well equipped' halls, which for all our wishes, may not be forthcoming for years. I do not conform to the view that such halls are an essential pre-requisite to the growth of theatre in this country. Over-elaboration of technical devices and an increasing dependence on them, in the given conditions here, is more likely to retard the growth of theatre and confine it to a groove that may not let it expand into new and original shapes through its own dynamism.[37]

As we can now note in hindsight, this is a selective and simple formulation of the fundamental principles that inform the Polish director Jerzy Grotowski's enormously influential theory of the 'poor theatre', which

> gives up the trappings used in the other visual arts. It is a theatre that concentrates on human actions only, and the relationship between the actors and the audience. It gives up all conventional stage effects . . . because they are not essential. . . . We wish to confront our art without costly devices or commercial accoutrements.[38]

In post-Independence Indian theatre, the full impact of
Grotowski's innovations appears in Bengali playwright Badal
Sircar's theory of the 'Third Theatre'—a contemporaneous
style with which Rakesh has little in common. But it is
interesting to note, in Rakesh's essays, the same anti-
technology, anti-capitalist stance that informs not only
Grotowski's avant-garde European practice but also the
postcolonial performance economies negotiated since the late
1950s by leading African and Caribbean playwrights such as
Wole Soyinka, Ngũgĩ wa Thiong'o, and Derek Walcott.

Ashadh ka ek din precedes by a few years the systematic
elaboration of these ideas in Rakesh's criticism, but it
embodies his core theoretical vision to an extraordinary
extent. From both literary and theatrical standpoints, the
play's most celebrated feature is its diction, a unique and
perfect medium that simultaneously evokes the classical and
the contemporary, and sustains the period atmosphere while
maintaining a quality of natural but cultured communication.
Satyadev Dubey pointed out that the play's 'modernity was
not allowed to encroach on the "poetry" of the situation
which had been crystallized in dialogues which startled the
Hindi world with their austere musicality. Though the Hindi
used was Sanskritized for the sake of the period, yet the play
brought to the Hindi language a fully-evolved dramatic idiom,
flawless in its speech rhythms and [possessing] a distinct
modern ring.'[39] Another director, Vivekdutt Jha, regarded
Rakesh's ability to get his meaning across to ordinary viewers
while negotiating a Sanskritized diction as his greatest success,
and one of the play's major strengths. Indeed, so vital is the
linguistic medium to the play's emotional effects that when

author-critic Kanhaiyalal Nandan saw the Theatre Group's 1972 English production in Bombay, which had used Sarah K. Ensley's translation, he felt that the empathy and delicacy of emotion associated with Kalidas's character 'were completely drowned out by the formal enunciation of a melodramatic English. . . . There was not even a remote sign here of Kalidas's emotional susceptibility and the profound inner conflict that should have consumed him at the end.'[40] The centrality of 'the dramatic word' to Rakesh's brand of theatre is fully borne out by this vital role of the language of original composition—not surprisingly, among the leading plays by the playwrights of Rakesh's generation, *Ashadh* has been the one performed least frequently in translation.

The visual–material aspects of staging also support the minimalism Rakesh advocates in the theatre. The single, simple set (conceived in part to reduce production costs) lends itself equally to indoor and outdoor performance. As the action unfolds, the passage of time and Mallika's deteriorating circumstances are denoted by a few strategic changes to the material environment representing her home. The scattered copies of Kalidas's works she has purchased over the years, and the blank pages she has sewn together for his future compositions, become the ordinary yet powerful symbols of her abandonment. The sociocultural contrasts between the villagers and courtiers are easily manifest in their styles of dress and delivery. Faisal Alkazi's 1972 production for Ruchika (New Delhi) emphasized the differences by employing a thoroughly artificial manner, rich costumes, heavy ornaments, intricate hairdos, and exaggerated make-up for the various courtly characters, while the villagers wore simple, faded earth tones and no make-up. The atmospheric elements that create the distinctive ambience of the play—the village setting, mountains, valleys, the sound of horses' hooves, and, most of all, the rain—are evoked mainly through the dialogue rather than shown. In short, no extraneous devices interfere with the patterns of sympathy and antipathy that the principal characters enact through their measured dialogue, or with the emotionally wrenching arc of the failed relationship between Mallika and Kalidas.

Ashadh ka ek din in Performance

For a work that permanently altered the landscape of post-Independence drama and theatre, *Ashadh* had a rather unsteady beginning as a stage vehicle. The preface to the second edition expresses Rakesh's dismay that no productions had materialized until then. The first performance-related reference appears in an entry in his diary dated 5 November 1958, which mentions that Ramesh Pal's group Rangmanch had received a grant from the Uttar Pradesh government to support a production in Lucknow in mid-December that year. The entry for 6 February 1959 contains an unconfirmed report that a performance of the play had also taken place at the annual political convention of the Congress party in Nagpur (held from 9–11 January 1959), but confirms that Pal's group performed it in Lucknow on 10 January. The performance of 21 January 1959 by Rangmanch, also in Lucknow, was part of a Hindi play festival, and the award it received for Best Production at this competition prefigured Rakesh's Sangeet Natak Akademi award for Best Play later in the year. This second award caught the attention of the up-and-coming actor-director Shyamanand Jalan in Calcutta, but his group Anamika had serious doubts about the viability of the work in performance. It was Jalan's adamant belief in the play's stage-worthiness, and his insistence on directing it, that took his production forward and launched the extraordinary performance history of *Ashadh ka ek din*. Like Rakesh's two other full-length plays, and comparable plays by other contemporary playwrights, *Ashadh* displays the main features that have marked iconic works for the post-Independence stage—an unbroken succession of major productions by noted directors in multiple urban locations, and translation into other Indian languages as well as English for publication and performance, around the country and abroad. In fact, the play is prominent among the contemporary works that democratically span the full spectrum of performative circumstances, from college and university dramatic societies and amateur groups to high-cultural institutions and leading theatre professionals.

The decades of the 1960s and 1970s were particularly important in establishing *Ashadh* in the national repertory. Jalan's pioneering 1960 production in Calcutta, the stronghold of Bengali theatre, was an unexpected venue for a new Hindi play by a relatively unknown author, and a bold step forward in the development of Hindi theatre in this eastern Indian metropolis. Ebrahim Alkazi's 1962 production for the National School of Drama, New Delhi, was his first as the school's newly appointed director. It gave the play a prestigious premier in the capital city, and connected the leading roles of Kalidas and Mallika with the two actors—Om Shivpuri and Sudha Sharma (later Shivpuri)—who were to play them with legendary success and remain associated with them for more than a decade. The first major production in Bombay was for Theatre Unit by Satyadev Dubey, a vocal admirer who described the play as a 'revolutionary breakaway' from the playwriting of the past, and a work that had 'electrified the literary and theatrical circles'.[41] There were many other notable productions outside these metropolitan locations, including those directed by Mohan Maharshi in Jaipur (1968), by Vivekdutt Jha in Sagar (1972) and Raipur (1975), by Bhanu Bharati in Udaipur (1975), and by Satish Chand and Bansi Kaul in Dehradun (1976). In Delhi, Maharshi directed the play again for the group Yatrik in 1970, while Sudha Shivpuri reprised her role as Mallika, and Om Shivpuri played Vilom in the 1973 production by their own theatre group, Dishantar. Other prominent productions in Delhi followed in 1981, 1983, and 1992, directed respectively by Amal Allana for Studio 1, Rajinder Nath for the Shri Ram Centre Repertory Company, and Ram Gopal Bajaj for the National School of Drama Repertory Company.

These productions were all in Hindi, the language in which (as we have learnt) the play makes its greatest impact, but the record of its multilingual dispersal through translation is significant in its own right. Joy Michael, a leading figure in English-language Indian theatre, took Sarah K. Ensley's translation to Mary Washington College, Virginia, as early as 1968. Within India, the first major English productions (also using Ensley's translation) were by Faisal Alkazi for the group Ruchika in New Delhi, and by Sam Kerawalla for Theatre Group in Bombay, both in 1972. During the same year, B.R. Nagesh and K.V. Subbanna directed the first two Kannada productions, Nagesh for the Kannada Sahitya Kala Sangh in Bangalore, and Subbanna for NINASAM, the nationally prominent theatre organization based in Heggodu, Karnataka (Akshara K.V. revived the play in Kannada for NINASAM Tirugata in 1991). An Assamese adaptation appeared on the stage in Gauhati (now spelt Guwahati) in 1976, and a Punjabi translation was directed by Ram Gopal Bajaj in Patiala in 1980 and in Delhi in 1984. The Manipuri production by Ratan Thiyam's Chorus Repertory Theatre in Imphal (1981) deserves special mention, because Thiyam maintained the stark modernity and realism of *Ashadh ka ek din* despite its divergence from his internationally celebrated style of richly choreographed total theatre, grounded in traditional regional styles of music, dance, and martial arts. The play was also translated into Gujarati in 1979 and Malayalam in 1984. Productions were staged in Marathi in 1976 and 1981, and in 2013 noted director and film-maker Atul Pethe premiered a new Marathi translation in Pune, which was on tour as of this writing in mid-2014. Our translation of the play is the most recent one in English. As noted in the Preface, it was commissioned by Neil Scharnick of Carthage College (Kenosha, Wisconsin) in August 2009, and produced there under his direction in March 2010. Needless to say, this information about the play's stage history, both in Hindi and in translation, is merely the tip of the iceberg in terms of its stage presence, because the frequency with which it is revived by amateur groups of all kinds, in India and the global Indian diaspora, is impossible to estimate.

Jaidev Taneja's admirable documentation of major productions in multiple languages does reveal some of the cruxes that determine the effectiveness of specific performances.[42] As Rakesh had intuited in the preface to the second edition of *Ashadh*, the roles of Kalidas, Mallika, and Vilom require seasoned actors, and Ambika should certainly be added to this list. Controlled, suggestive, and multilayered performances in these roles are vital for anchoring the play as a whole, which otherwise runs the risk of sliding into romanticism, sentimentalism, melodrama, or mere pathos. In Anamika's 1960 production, the four parts were created with notable success by Jalan, Sunita Railin (later Bhagat), Badri Tiwari, and noted theatre personality Pratibha Agrawal, respectively, though the emotional poignancy of Railin's performance was dominant: according to Agrawal, its memory even years later moved 'not only the eyes but the soul to tears'.[43] In 1962, the performances by Om Shivpuri, Sudha Sharma, Arun Agnihotri, and Meena Williams in the same roles at the National School of Drama established a collective standard that has not been surpassed for this play, just as that production as a whole remains a triumph for Ebrahim Alkazi, and a touchstone for post-Independence Indian theatre in general.

Among the later productions, however, even some of the best efforts have exposed a variety of fault lines. Satyadev Dubey as Vilom and Amrish Puri as Matul were outstanding in Dubey's 1964 production, but Rekha Sabnis's Mallika was distressingly immature, and flattened the play's serious resonances. Dishantar's 1973 production took full advantage of Sudha Shivpuri's re-presentation as Mallika, but because of the focus on her suffering, the broader sociopolitical concerns of the play became secondary. The tempo and movement in Studio 1's 1981 production was reportedly hampered by

Nissar Allana's large realistic set, which included trees, plants, bushes, and a bridge. Alkazi had been conspicuously successful with the outdoor set he had designed in 1962 to place *Ashadh* outside the proscenium, but the same choice on the part of Mohan Maharshi failed in 1970 in the same city because of colder weather and faulty acoustics.

Every significant production has demonstrated, in fact, that the actual visual–material arrangement of the mise en scène and the 'look' of the characters are integral to the play's impact, leading to an interesting paradox. On philosophical and cultural grounds, Rakesh had asserted his authorial right to remake history in the image of the present, but in performance the play's visual and aural qualities have returned it powerfully to history. No major director has ignored Rakesh's meticulous stage directions regarding the atmosphere, shape, texture, and arrangement of the spaces and objects constituting the mise en scène: a rustic chamber replete with the signs and symbols of Hindu antiquity, such as painted swastikas and lotuses, small clay lamps, metal utensils covered with *kusha* grass, and a tiger skin thrown over a low seat. Vivekdutt Jha noted that recreating Kalidas's period on stage in his Sagar production required an exceptional amount of labour, and it was vital for every physical object to be in its proper place during the staging.[44] In his 1972 production, Faisal Alkazi 'saw the play in terms of some special visual–aural images': by integrating light and sound with the material–human environment, he created vivid tableaux that both heightened and framed the play's moments of emotional crisis, and became indelibly imprinted in his mind.[45] The successful evocation of antiquity, through set design, in the Ebrahim Alkazi, Joy Michael, and

Kerawalla productions of 1962, 1968, and 1972, respectively, also came in for specific praise from reviewers. The loyalty of stage directors to Rakesh's imagined environment extends to costumes as well: there has been no major production of *Ashadh* so far in modern dress. The styles of costume vary from the simple to the exotic and even the ascetic, but the characters' obvious physical dissonance with the contemporary urban Indian (or Western) spectator—a version of estrangement— marks them as 'different' even as their predicaments assume familiar qualities.

Because the relationship between Kalidas and Mallika is the emotional–existential core of the play, its extraordinary entanglement with the creative lives of Om and Sudha Shivpuri is also a notable aspect of its performance history. 'I probably cannot describe in words how close that character is to me even today, which I was living through when I performed the role of Mallika,' Sudha Shivpuri wrote in a 1992 memoir.[46] Both she and Om Shivpuri were National School of Drama graduates and founder members of the school's Repertory Company, for which they played the lead roles in Karnad's *Tughlaq*, Rakesh's *Laharon ke rajhans*, and Sophocles' *Antigone*—all in 1966. But while Om Shivpuri went on to a successful and visible career as a serious character actor in Indian 'middle' cinema and commercial Bombay cinema, his wife remained principally a stage actress with a regional audience. (Her success as the matriarch 'Ba' in the Hindi television serial *Kyunki saas bhi kabhi bahu thi* [Because the Mother-in-Law Also Was Once a Daughter-in-Law], which ran from 2000 to 2008, followed a decade after Om Shivpuri's death in 1990.) When asked about her feelings regarding this disparity in their professional profiles, Sudha Shivpuri claims to have repeated the lines from Rakesh's play in which Mallika expresses stark despair at the news that Kalidas has abandoned his life at the imperial court:

> Even though I didn't remain in your life, you've always been an enduring part of my life. I never let you grow distant from me. You went on creating, and I continued to think that I was meaningful—that my life, too, has accomplished something. . . . And today, will you reduce my life to meaninglessness in this way? . . . You may be detached from life, but I can't be detached from it now. Can you look at life with my eyes? Do you know how these years of my life have been spent? What I've been witness to? What I was, and what I've become? [see pp. 167–68]

For a decade in the stage life of the play, the emotional drama and tragic unravelling of the Kalidas–Mallika relationship acquired even greater intensity through this association with the actors' lives, and the retrospective text of Shivpuri's memoir recaptures that poignancy: 'Today, when Mohan Rakesh is no longer with us and his Kalidas has also left me alone and gone away, become disengaged from life, once again I remember those same lines from *Ashadh ka ek din* and console myself.'[47]

Shivpuri's experience is another sign of the interpenetration of art and life, past and present, which this play represents more than any other work by Rakesh, dramatic or fictional. The play, however, is more than the sum of its parts: given Rakesh's interest in revitalizing the Hindi stage through modernist experimentation, the real vindication of his

unorthodox methods ultimately lies in the intense excitement
that *Ashadh* has generated among theatre professionals and
critics ever since its first appearance. Jalan's production was
described as having given the Hindi stage 'an entirely new
scope and qualitative standard'; Alkazi's was credited with
transforming 'not only the condition but the direction of the
Hindi stage'.[48] Like Namvar Singh, Satyadev Dubey felt that
the play had 'elevated playwriting to an enviable top position.
So far it had only been a poor relation of the other literary
forms, but now it commanded a new respect in spite of being
the least remunerative.'[49] Such appraisals validate Rakesh's
radical positions on history, tradition, canonicity, and creativity,
but remarks by directors and performers also suggest that
these thematic emphases have formed an important part of
their own respective approaches to the play's communicable
meanings. As Jha observes (echoing Rakesh and voicing the
majority view among theatre professionals), Indian culture
tends to idealize tradition and deny signs of vulnerability in
its icons, but 'by presenting Kalidas along with his weaknesses
on stage, the playwright has made an important contribution
towards the breaking of traditional modes of thinking in
society'.[50] The quality and regional reception of the 2010–11
student production at Carthage College in the United States
confirms for us that the magic of the play's dialogue, and
its profound ability to move audiences across cultures and
languages, remains intact.

A Geography of the Play

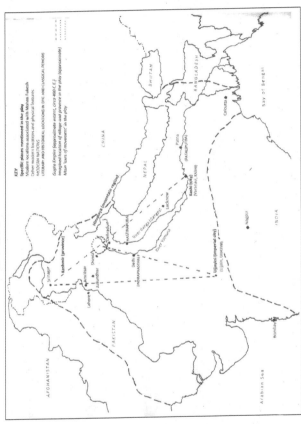

This map superposes the imaginative geography of Mohan Rakesh's *Ashadh ka ek din* on contemporary India. The places in the play (in bold) are set against literary and historical places in the epic and classical periods (small capitals), places significant in Rakesh's life (roman), and other modern locations (light face). Within the Gupta empire's approximate boundaries (outer broken line), the play's offstage movements occur on two 'nested triangles': Ujjayini–Kashmir–village (dotted circle), and Ujjayini–Kashmir–Kashi.

Mohan Rakesh: A Chronology

This is a detailed chronology of Rakesh's life and work, based on the most reliable biographical and bibliographical information available. Since his writings have an exceptional afterlife in several genres, the list also includes posthumous publications over a period of four decades. In bibliographic entries, the language of the text is Hindi and the place of publication is either Delhi or New Delhi, unless noted otherwise. For various Indian cities and states, we have retained the names current at the time mentioned; hence 'Bombay' or 'Calcutta', rather than the once-and-future 'Mumbai' or 'Kolkata'. After their first occurrences, the names of Rakesh's main publishers are abbreviated to their principal terms: for example, 'Rajpal and Sons' to 'Rajpal', and 'Radhakrishna Prakashan' to 'Radhakrishna'. While focusing on Rakesh, this chronology also offers unexpected glimpses of literary canon formation in Hindi and India; of the dissemination of Indian-language literatures beyond their own borders; and the consolidation of print readership in an age of audio, visual, and electronic media.

1925   Rakesh is born on 8 January in Amritsar (Punjab), to Karam Chand Arora (Guglani) and Bachchan Kaur. Birth-name: Madan Mohan Guglani; adopts the nom de plume 'Mohan Rakesh' as a young adult.

1941   Father dies, leaving Rakesh with the primary responsibility for his mother and two siblings.

1942–47   Education at Punjab University, Lahore (now in Pakistan); a bachelor's degree in English literature, followed by a master's degree in Sanskrit literature.

1947   Begins appointment as lecturer in Hindi at Elphinstone College, Bombay.

1949   *Satya aur kalpana: chhah ekanki* (Truth and Imagination: Six One-Act Plays), published by Motilal Banarsidass.

          Compelled to resign position at Elphinstone College due to very poor eyesight (a lifelong affliction of extreme myopia).

1949–50   Lecturer in Hindi at D.A.V. College, Jalandhar. Loses job within six months for his participation in the activities of the Teachers' Union.

1950   *Insan ke khandahar* (The Ruins of Human Beings), Rakesh's first collection of short stories in Hindi, published by Pragati Prakashan.

          Marries Sushila Meherwal in Allahabad on 10 December.

1950–52   Teacher at Bishop Cotton School, Simla.

1952   Master's degree in Hindi literature from Punjab University, Jalandhar.

1953   Reappointed at D.A.V. College, Jalandhar, as head of the Hindi department.

         Akhiri chattan tak (Up to the Final Rockface), an account of travels along India's western coast, published by Pragati.

         Jo kahen papa jo karen papa (Whatever Papa Says, Whatever Papa Does), translation into Hindi by Rakesh of Clarence Day's collection of humorous sketches, *Life with Father* (1920).

1956   *Amar-jyoti: mahan vyaktiyon ke jivan ki jhalak* (The Immortal Flame: A Glimpse of the Lives of Great Men), co-authored by Rakesh and Inder Nath Madan, published by Hindi Bhavan, Jalandhar.

         Son Navneet born on 8 May.

1957   *Naye badal* (New Clouds), Rakesh's second collection of short stories, published by Bharatiya Jnanapith in Kashi.

         '*Sahitya rachana: anubhuti se abhivyakti tak*' ('Literary Composition: From Sensation and Feeling to Representation'), essay by Rakesh, also published in English translation as 'Intuition and Expression in Literature' in the *Research Bulletin (Arts)* of the University of the Punjab, no. 22 (Hoshiarpur). Reprinted the same year as a small pamphlet by Vishveshvaranand Book Agency, Hoshiarpur.

Resigns from D.A.V. College, Jalandhar. Divorce from his first wife, Sushila Meherwal, finalized in Pathankot on 9 August.

1958   *Janvar aur janvar* (Animal and Animal), Rakesh's third collection of short stories, published by Rajkamal Prakashan.

Ashadh ka ek din (One Day in the Season of Rain), Rakesh's first full-length play, published by Rajpal and Sons in June. Second edition published in September.

1960   Marries Pushpa Chopra, his second wife, in Kullu on 11 May.

Accepts position as lecturer in Hindi at Delhi University to teach evening classes, but resigns in October, after just two months.

Panch lambi kahaniyan (Five Long Stories) a collection of Rakesh's longer stories; publisher unknown.

Us rat ke bad (After That Night), Rakesh's Hindi translation of Graham Greene's English novel, *The End of the Affair*, published by Rajkamal Paperbacks.

1961   *Ek aur zindagi* (One More Life), Rakesh's fourth collection of short stories, published by Rajpal. Contains a preface by Rakesh, *'Kahani: naye sandarbhon ki khoj'* ('The Short Story: A Search for New Contexts').

Andhere band kamare (Dark Sealed Rooms), Rakesh's first novel, published by Rajkamal.

Mrichchhakatika (The Little Clay Cart), Rakesh's translation of the Sanskrit play by Shudraka, published by Rajkamal.

Separates from his second wife, Pushpa Chopra.

1962   Begins work as editor of Hindi literary magazine *Sarika*, on 9 March in Bombay.

1963   Resigns from editorship of *Sarika* and returns to Delhi in March.

Marries Anita Aulak in a *gandharva* ceremony in Delhi on 22 July. The couple elope to Bombay on 29 July, and announce the marriage at a celebration with friends on 3 August.

Laharon ke rajhans (The Royal Swans of the Waves), Rakesh's second full-length play, published by Rajkamal.

1964   Rakesh and Anita return to Delhi and settle there.

Shreshtha kahaniyan (Outstanding Stories), five stories by Rakesh selected by Kamleshwar, published by Rajpal in their series titled *Naye kahanikar* (New Storytellers).

1965   *Shakuntal*, Rakesh's Hindi translation of Kalidas's Sanskrit play, *Abhijnana-shakuntala*, published by Radhakrishna.

Ayine ke samne (Before the Mirror), a collection of self-portraits by prominent Hindi writers, edited by Rakesh, published by Akshara Prakashan.

Rat ki bahon men (In the Arms of the Night), a collection of creative non-fiction on the subject of the city edited by Rakesh, published by Radhakrishna.

Hiroshima ke phool (The Flowers of Hiroshima), Rakesh's translation into Hindi of Edita Morris's landmark German novel, *Die Blumen von Hiroshima* (1959), published by Rajkamal.

1966   *Faulad ka akash* (The Sky of Steel), Rakesh's fifth collection of short stories, published by Akshara.

1967   *Parivesh* (Frames of Reference), a collection of essays by Rakesh, published by Bharatiya Jnanapith, Calcutta.

           Daughter Purva born on 28 October.

1967–69   Stories from Rakesh's five original collections (1950, 1957, 1958, 1961, 1966), along with some new stories selected by him, reprinted in four volumes by Radhakrishna. These volumes are now titled *Aj ke saye* (Today's Shadows, 1967), *Royen reshe* (Fibres and Filaments, 1968), *Ek-ek duniya* (Each and Every World, 1969), and *Mile-jule chehare* (Mixed and Mingled Faces, 1969).

1968   *Na anevala kal* (The Tomorrow That Never Arrives), Rakesh's second novel, published by Rajpal.

Laharon ke rajhans, Rakesh's second full-length play originally published in 1963, appears in a substantially revised third edition from Rajkamal.

1969   *Adhe adhure* (Half Formed, Half Unfinished), Rakesh's last full-length play to be completed in his lifetime, published by Radhakrishna.

One Day in Ashadh, Sarah K. Ensley's English translation of *Ashadh ka ek din* (1958), publisher not specified.

1970   Son Shaleen born on 12 November.

Panch parde: panch ekankiyon ka sangraha (Five Curtains: A Collection of Five One-Act Plays), edited by Rakesh and published by Radhakrishna.

Lingering Shadows, Jai Ratan's English translation of Rakesh's first novel, *Andhere band kamare* (1961) published by Hind Pocket Books.

Shreshtha kahaniyan: naye kahanikar (Outstanding Short Stories: New Storytellers), a selection of stories by Rakesh, Rajendra Yadav, and Kamleshwar, published by Rajpal.

Uski roti (His Bread), Mani Kaul's film based on Rakesh's short story of the same title, released by the National Film Development Corporation, Bombay.

1971   Rakesh receives two-year Nehru Fellowship, and begins extensive schedule of travel abroad and work on monograph in English, *The Dramatic Word*.

Meri priya kahaniyan (My Favourite Stories), a selection of ten of his stories, chosen by Rakesh, published by Rajpal.

Half-Way House, Bindu Batra's English version of *Adhe adhure*, published in the journal *Enact*, edited by Rajinder Paul.

Mani Kaul's film based on *Ashadh ka ek din* (One Day in the Season of Rain) released by the National Film Development Corporation, Bombay.

1972   *Antaral* (Interval), Rakesh's third and last novel, published by Rajkamal.

Char khandon men prakashit mohan rakesh ki samagra kahaniyan (The Complete Short Stories of Mohan Rakesh, Published in Four Volumes), published by Rajpal. This edition, separate from the four-volume edition of 1967–69 published by Radhakrishna, initially contained three volumes. These volumes were titled *Quarter*, *Pehchan* (Acquaintance), and *Waris* (The Heir), respectively, and each also carried the title of the set as an announcement on its title page. The fourth volume, containing twelve stories collected for the first time posthumously and edited by Kamleshwar, was published in 1974, but is misdated 1972. See the 1974 entry below on *Ek ghatana*.

Mad Delight: A Scattering of Words, Sounds, and Visuals, English translation of Rakesh's 'backstage play', *Chhatriyan* (Umbrellas), published in Delhi. Publisher not specified.

Samaya-sarathi (Time's Charioteer), short biographies by Rakesh of twelve exceptional personalities of the past 2500 years, and a discussion of the principal mentalities of the Common Era. Published by Radhakrishna.

Dies suddenly of cardiac arrest on 3 December. Anita Rakesh becomes her late husband's literary executor.

1972–73   Mohan Rakesh Memorial Issues appear in the following periodicals: *Natarang* (December 1972, ed. Nemichandra Jain); *Enact* (January–February 1973, ed. Rajinder Paul); *Sarika* (March 1973, ed. Kamleshwar); *Journal of South Asian Literature* (vol. 9.2–3 [1973], ed. Carlo Coppola).

1973   *Ande ke chhilke, anya ekanki tatha bij natak* (Eggshells, Other One-Act Plays, and Seed Plays), a collection of seven short plays by Rakesh, published by Radhakrishna.

Short Plays of Mohan Rakesh, a collection of four plays in English translation, published in Delhi. Publisher not specified.

1973–75   *Chand sataren aur* (A Few Lines More), Anita Rakesh's memoir of the time before, during, and after her life with Rakesh; initially published in serial form in the literary magazine *Sarika* (which had an old association with Rakesh, who edited it in 1962–63); published as a book by Radhakrishna in 1975.

1974   *Rat bitane tak tatha anya dhvani natak* ('Till the Night
            Has Passed' and Other Plays for Voices), a collection
            of eight radio plays, published by Radhakrishna.

            Bakalam khud (With My Own Pen), a collection of
            Rakesh's essays and articles, published by Rajpal.

            Bina hada-mans ke adami (Men without Flesh and
            Bones), a collection of four short stories by Rakesh
            for juvenile readers, published by Radhakrishna.

            *Ek ghatana: lekhak ki pustak-akar men pahali bar
            prakashit barah kahaniyan* (An Incident: Twelve
            Stories by the Author Published in Book Form for
            the First Time). This is the fourth volume in the new
            set of collected stories, three volumes of which were
            published by Rajpal in 1972 (see above). This volume
            is edited, with a preface, by Kamleshwar.

            *Anthology: Thirteen Stories, Self-Portrait, An Interview,
            and Adhe-adhure*; publication in book form, by
            Radhakrishna, of the Mohan Rakesh Special Issue of
            Journal of South Asian Literature (1973) noted above.

1975   *Pair tale ki zamin* (The Ground beneath One's Feet),
            Rakesh's unfinished full-length play, completed by
            Kamleshwar and published by Rajpal. (The title is
            echoed in Salman Rushdie's sixth novel, *The Ground
            beneath Her Feet* [1999], and by the lyrics of a song in
            it, which the popular band U2 recorded later.)

            Mohan rakesh: sahityik aur sanskritik drishti (Mohan
            Rakesh: The Literary and Cultural Vision), a

volume of Rakesh's uncollected essays, published by Radhakrishna; with an Introduction by film-maker Basu Bhattacharya.

Tétova árnyak, Peter Balaban's Hungarian translation of Rakesh's first novel, *Andhere band kamare* (1961), published by Europa in Budapest. The Hungarian title means 'Lingering Shadows', indicating that this version is based on Jai Ratan's 1970 English translation of the novel, and not on the Hindi original.

1976   *Pahila raja* (The First King), a volume published by the National Book Trust, containing Marathi translations, by important playwrights, of two modern Hindi plays: P.L. Deshpande's rendering of Jagdishchandra Mathur's *Pahala raja*, and Vijay Tendulkar's version of Rakesh's *Adhe adhure* (1969).

1979   *Pahelo raja* (The First King), a volume published by the National Book Trust, containing Kirtikant Seth's Gujarati translation of two modern Hindi plays: Rakesh's *Adhe adhure* (titled *Ardham adhuram*) and Jagdishchandra Mathur's *Pahala raja*. See entry for 1976 above.

Ashadhano ek divas, Bhagvati Kumar Sharma's Gujarati translation of *Ashadh ke ek din* (1958), published by Kumkum Prakashan, Ahmedabad.

1980   *Alegalalli rajahamsagalu*, Siddhalinga Pattanashetti's Kannada translation of Rakesh's second full-length play, *Laharon ke rajhans* (1963), published by Ananya Prakashan in Mysore.

1982   *Temnuie Zakrituie Kaminatui*, L. Kuznetsov's Russian
          translation of Rakesh's first novel, *Andhere band
          kamare* (1961), published by Khudozhestvennaya
          Literatura, Moscow.

1983   *Hua jia de qi zi*, Zhong Yi's Chinese translations of
          a selection of Rakesh's short stories, published in
          Nanchang, China.

1984   *Pratinidhi kahaniyan* (Representative Stories), a
          collection of eight of Rakesh's stories, edited by
          Mohan Gupta, published by Rajkamal Paperbacks.

          Mohan rakesh ki sampurna kahaniyan (The Complete
          Short Stories of Mohan Rakesh), published by
          Rajpal. This is a one-volume edition of the
          publisher's earlier four-volume set of 1972–74, and
          contains sixty-six stories. Its Appendix 1 lists the
          contents of the five original collections of short
          stories, published between 1950 and 1966 (fifty
          stories in all); Appendix 2 contains Kamleshwar's
          short preface to the 1974 volume of twelve
          uncollected stories (see above).

          Ashadhatille oru divasam, Malayalam translation of
          Ashadh ka ek din (1958) published by National Book
          Stall, Kottayam.

1985   *Mohan rakesh ki dayari* (The Diary of Mohan Rakesh),
          published by Rajpal. Contains a preface by Rakesh,
          'Apni dayari ke bare men swayam' ('About My Diary,
          from Me'); a preface by Anita Rakesh, *'Rakeshji ki
          yeh dayari'* ('This Diary by Rakesh'); and a preface by

Kamleshwar, *'Dayariyan: ek lekhak ka apna registan'* ('Diaries: A Writer's Own Desert').

1987   *Barah sau chhabbis bata sat* (Twelve Hundred and Twenty-six by Seven), Jitendra Mittal's dramatic adaptation in Hindi of Rakesh's short story, *'Paramatma ka kutta'* ('God's Dog'), published by Vani Prakashan.

1989   *Les Bienheureuses*, a collection of Hindi short stories translated into French by Nicole Balbir, published in Paris by L'Harmattan; contains Rakesh's short story *'Suhaginen'* ('The Fortunate Married Women'), translated as the volume's title story, *'Les Bienheureuses'*.

        Yakeato no aruji, Toshio Tanaka's Japanese translation of Rakesh's work, published by Mekon, Tokyo. Further information unavailable.

1990   *Sahitya aur sanskriti: nibandha* (Literature and Culture: Essays), published by Radhakrishna.

        Grosstadtgeschichten (Stories of the Big City), Konrad Meisig's German translation of a selection of Rakesh's stories, published by Otto Harrassowitz in Wiesbaden, Germany.

1993   *Mohan rakesh ke sampurna natak* (The Complete Plays of Mohan Rakesh), edited by Nemichandra Jain, published by Rajpal. This is the standard edition that we have used for our translation of *Ashadh ka ek din* (1958).

Another Life and Other Stories: Translated from the Hindi, a collection of eleven stories by Rakesh rendered by various hands, published by Rupa Paperbacks.

1995   *Rakesh aur parivesh: patron men* (Rakesh and His Circle: In Letters), a selection of Rakesh's correspondence, edited by Jaidev Taneja and published by Radhakrishna.

1996   *To the Vanishing Point*, Shyla Elizabeth Osborn's English translation of Rakesh's early travelogue, *Akhiri chattan tak* (1953), completed as MFA thesis at the University of Iowa.

1998   *Ekatra: aprakashita-asankalita rachanayen* (Gathered Together: Unpublished and Uncollected Writings), a collection of reminiscences, travel writings, essays, early one-act plays, novellas, diary excerpts, and fragments of stories and plays, edited by Jaidev Taneja and published by Radhakrishna.

2000   *Punashcha: mohan rakesh aur ashk dampati ka patrachar, 1951–1969* (Postscript: The Correspondence Between Mohan Rakesh and the Ashk Couple, 1951–1969), edited by Jaidev Taneja, published by Radhakrishna.

2001   *Rakesh samagra* (Rakesh Complete), a selection of Rakesh's works, edited by Nandkishore Naval, published by Vani Prakashan.

2002   *Das pratinidhi kahaniyan* (Ten Representative Stories) by Rakesh, edited by Jaidev Taneja and published by Kitab Ghar.

2003   *Natya-vimarsha* (Reflections on Theatre), Rakesh's collected essays on drama and theatre, edited by Jaidev Taneja and published by the National School of Drama.

        Mere sakshatkar (My Face-to-Face Testimonials), a collection of Rakesh's interviews, edited by Jaidev Taneja and published by Kitab Ghar.

2004   *Dvidala*, the leading playwright P.L. Deshpande's Marathi translations of Badal Sircar's Bengali play *Sara ratir* (All Night), and Mohan Rakesh's short play *Kadachit* (Perhaps); published by Mauj Prakashan Griha, Mumbai.

2007   'The Owner of Rubble', Alok Bhalla's English translation of Rakesh's short story *'Malbe ka malik'*, appears in *Manoa* 19:1, a journal published by the University of Hawaii Press.

2008   *Purvabhyas: arambhik ekanki* (Beginning Exercises: Early One-Act Plays), edited by Jaidev Taneja, published by Rajkamal.

2010   *Mohan rakesh sanchayan* (Mohan Rakesh: Selections), a selection of short stories, plays, essays, and other works, edited by Ravindra Kaliya and Kunal Singh, published by Bharatiya Jnanapith.

        Stories: Translated from the Hindi, a selection of five stories by Rakesh in English translation, published by Grassroots in Bhubaneswar, Orissa.

2011   *Mohan rakesh rachanavali* (The Works of Mohan
              Rakesh), a thirteen-volume set edited by Jaidev
              Taneja, published by Radhakrishna.

Translators' Note

Ashadh ka ek din is written in modern Hindi prose, but its outstanding characteristics are its poetic use of language and its superbly modulated atmosphere. On the page and in the theatre, the play foregrounds a fusion of dialogue, stage directions, and dramatic action (a synthesis of diegesis and mimesis), a capacity to immerse its audience in a variety of emotions, and an extraordinary range of aesthetic techniques and dramatic effects. Beneath these qualities lies the depth of Rakesh's characterization, which is displayed in his conception and treatment of diverse fictional characters, especially Mallika, Kalidas, and Vilom; and in his representation of women, particularly his handling of Ambika and 'the tragedy of Mallika'.[1] Underneath these particulars, we find more abstract components: his thematization of the life and work of the classical poet Kalidas, and of the dilemmas of writers in any period of history; his theory and practice of drama and theatrecraft in general; and his distinctive, self-reflexive modernist classicism. All these qualities converge to emphasize the play's literariness—some early readers of the first edition, in fact, expressed doubts about its performability, particularly in relation to Act Three. A translator who wishes to transpose *Ashadh* into another medium consequently has to invent ways of producing a verbal artefact that parallels the Hindi original in craft, while also rendering it as a play for performance in unfamiliar environments.

At the most practical level, the translator's effort has to focus first on doing justice to Rakesh's text as an aesthetic object. The ideal of translation on this plane is the literary one, which runs from John Dryden to Paul Valéry to A.K. Ramanujan, and postulates figuratively that 'only poems can translate poems'. If we look at this ideal through Ramanujan's lens, then the pursuit of a translation that displays high aesthetic skill is inevitably constrained by the fact that it is not an independent literary work, but an artefact that has to represent another artefact.[2] *Ashadh* presents itself as the kind of text of which neither an 'imitation' nor an 'adaptation' can be adequate: almost all the qualities for which Hindi readers and viewers value the play, and for which it remains a seminal phenomenon in Indian drama, are lost when a rendering fails to capture its verbal characteristics. A translator therefore has to confront the ideal of metaphrase, the process of 'turning an author word by word, and line by line, from one language into another'.[3] This constraint implies that the translator has to strive for a literal version of *Ashadh* that somehow also captures the poetry of the original.

In transpositions from Hindi to English, however, metaphrase is difficult to accomplish even without the pressure to achieve poetic value. In general, the technical properties of the two languages and their mutual differences—noun cases, systems of tenses, constructions of grammatical subject, uses of active, passive, and middle voice, and so on—make it extremely difficult to establish a one-to-one equation or equivalence at the level of individual words. An isolated Hindi word, for example, may require several English terms for its rendering, especially if its carries multiple meanings or nuances, but an entire Hindi phrase may be captured quite precisely by a single, resonant English word. Whether in verse or in prose, a close English version thus tends to expand and contract elastically in relation to a Hindi original, usually within a single sentence, making a word-by-word metaphrase a literal-minded impossibility.

In the specific case of *Ashadh*, literal translation as an end—rather than as a transitional means—tends to produce opaqueness and redundancy. In order to create a simulacrum of life in the classical period of India's literary and cultural history (circa 400–1200 CE), Rakesh develops a unique verbal medium for the play, which uses the syntax of modern Hindi but a vocabulary derived from Sanskrit, without the traces of Persian and Arabic that historically permeate the language in post-classical times. In the first half of Act One, for instance, Mallika, Ambika, Kalidas, and Dantul employ a range of words that have ancient Sanskrit roots but do not occur in modern conversational Hindi: among them, *upatyakayen* (foothills, lowlands, valleys), *talpa* (bed, couch, seat), *bhartsana* (reproach, menace, threat, curse, abuse), *sharkara* (sugar), *vitrishna* (repulsion, revulsion), *atma-pravanchana* (self-deception, delusion), *samudrik* (clairvoyance), *lanchhana* (taint, stigma, criticism, attack), and *pratadana* (scolding, berating, torment, disgrace, oppression, persecution).[4] Moreover, Rakesh integrates this linguistic register with a relatively formal diction, in Aristotle's sense of *lexis* (as both choice and arrangement of words, hence as style of expression); at the same time, he succeeds in shaping the dialogue as natural, free-flowing conversation among the characters, without resorting to modern colloquialisms.[5] This unusual, experimental combination of abstruse vocabulary and conversational ease is part of a double estrangement in the play at the level of language itself, which defamiliarizes modern Hindi with a pervasive classicism, even as it defamiliarizes the classical with an incursive modernity. As a result, the task of rendering the Sanskritized vocabulary accurately is no longer a task of word-by-word metaphrase, but one of inflecting the diction within a multilayered rendition of style and structure, without losing the particularity of etymology or semantic resonance.

As scholars and translators who study several languages and literatures between them, and are familiar with the conflicting demands of literary and literal translation, we approached this project as an active collaboration from the start. Despite the impossibility of literalism, we read and translated the play together between August and November 2009, word by word and sentence by sentence—for several hours a day, two to three times a week. Over the following months, we corrected and improved our draft sporadically; in the second week of February 2010, we sent Neil Scharnick a clean performance text for his production at Carthage College, to be staged five weeks later. We reviewed and revised the translation collaboratively once more in July and August 2014, collating different drafts and comparing them to the original as we prepared this volume for press. We did not expect the process of translation to be so long, but during this period we also explored Rakesh's other plays, as well as his novels, short stories, essays and interviews, diaries, correspondence, travel writings, and translations (from Sanskrit into Hindi), together with scholarship on his life and work in Hindi and English. These materials furnished the basis for our commentary on the author and the play, which appears in various forms throughout this book; to a commensurate extent, they also provided essential contexts for the final shape of our translation.

In this extended process, we resolved the tension between a *literal* and a *literary* rendering by shifting from the principle of 'word by word' equivalence to a more circumspect principle of inter-linearity—the 'line by line' portion of the formula—which means that phrases and sentences, rather than isolated words, served as the units of our translation. If a translation treats sentence length as an independent variable, then a sentence in English prose can convey most of what is said in a corresponding Hindi construction, even if one English word on its own cannot enclose all the nuances of one Hindi word. Thus, an English sentence, as a well-defined but flexible textual unit, can function as a comprehensive and reliable transposition of its Hindi counterpart, with the capacity to project multiple meanings. The version of *Ashadh* included in these pages aims for inclusive correspondences or parallels of this kind between Rakesh's verbal constructions in Hindi and our constructions in English, proceeding syntactically rather than lexically, metonymically rather than metaphorically. (Thus, to take a small example from the passage discussed below, we have Ambika say, 'Mallika, bring Matul a seat from the inner room', which represents the sequential or metonymic meaning of the Hindi sentence, rather than 'Mallika, bring Matul a chair from the bedroom', which would be an unhistorical and misleading metaphorical rendering.) In adopting this method, our translation follows Ramanujan's theory and practice in general, and swerves away from two alternatives: Walter Benjamin's paradigm, where 'words rather than sentences [prove] to be the primary element of the translator' (which is based on a scriptural hermeneutics of the Hebrew Bible, and on the limited examples of modern French and German); and Jacques Derrida's Benjaminian affirmation that translation requires a 'displacement' from 'the syntagmatic to the paradigmatic level' (which valorizes allegoresis, and does not work for imaginative literature).[6]

Even without M.M. Bakhtin's concepts of dialogism and heteroglossia, we know that sentences—like words—never occur in isolation, especially in the dialogue of a play, so Ramanujan's principle of structural or metonymic translation applies as much to longer passages as to clauses and phrases.[7] Since the larger verbal configurations in *Ashadh* are always significant units of composite meaning, they ultimately govern our rendering of sentences as parts nested inside a circumscribing whole. With larger discursive units, however, questions about grammar, word choice, etymology, denotation, and connotation give way to questions concerning tone, suggestion, mood, voice, and speaker's character. Rakesh's theatrecraft in *Ashadh* modulates the more rarefied effects of his prose with exceptional—and widely praised—poetic and rhetorical sophistication. Since he articulates these effects at higher levels of textual organization, we pay close attention to the tone of each passage and to the character who delivers it, on the page and in performance. We therefore seek to develop a distinctive voice for each character in English, which broadly regulates the tone of all the passages and sentences embedded in the dialogue assigned to him or her. At this level of coordination, our representations of tone and voice contribute not only to each character's identity or role in the play, but also to the overall communication of mood and atmosphere in the text—which is achieved, in the original, not by outright statement but by concerted suggestion and indirection. In *Ashadh*, the evolving mood of each character and situation, the cumulative tone of the interactions among various characters, and the metamorphosing atmosphere of the play are vital to its dramatic structure and manifold aesthetic effect.

Given the multilayered literariness and integrity of Rakesh's text, the best indicators of our method of representation may be two sample vignettes from the translation, which bring a range of techniques into play, from the small to the large. Towards the middle of Act One, readers and viewers encounter a secondary character named Matul, the fictionalized Kalidas's maternal uncle, who has been the poet's adoptive guardian since childhood and has raised him in the village where *Ashadh* is set, and in whose home the latter still lives as a young adult at this point in the play. At the start of the scene, Matul enters the home of Ambika and Mallika (the mise en scène) in excited and chaotic response to the act's 'inciting incident'—a delegation of royal courtiers, led by an acharya (a senior master-scholar), has just arrived in the village, to offer Kalidas the position of court poet, and to escort him back to the imperial city of Ujjayini for his inauguration. Following standard social etiquette, the acharya has contacted Matul, as head of household and as Kalidas's long-time guardian; responding spontaneously to this unexpected development, Matul has tried to locate Kalidas and give him the news; but the poet has rebuffed the honour, throwing his uncle into comical consternation. Matul leaves the acharya in the care of a younger villager and helpmate (a 'wing-man'), Nikshep, and turns up at Ambika and Mallika's door in 'a dishevelled state', seeking ways to put sense into Kalidas's head. While Matul is expostulating to the two women, Nikshep arrives to update Matul—as instructed—that the acharya has finished resting and is awaiting his host's return. After castigating Nikshep for leaving their distinguished guest unattended, Matul returns to his exasperation with Kalidas:

MATUL: . . . This man has no sense of even ordinary conduct with people, and you talk about his public relations. . . . His lordship was coming home with a fawn in his arms. Luckily, I spotted him just outside the house. I pleaded with him: 'O master of the tribe of poets, this is not the time to enter our home in such a state. A great scholar has come for you from Ujjayini, and is waiting for you.' As soon as he heard this, his lordship turned away. As though he'd seen a snake in his path.

> *Mallika sits down near Ambika on the window seat. Matul resumes pacing.*

AMBIKA: Mallika, bring Matul a seat from the inner room.

> *Mallika begins to rise, but Matul stops her.*

MATUL: No, I don't want a seat. The Acharya's waiting for me.

> *Nikshep looks at Ambika and smiles. Matul walks*
> *up to the end of the room and turns back.*

I said to him, 'O poet supreme, the Acharya's here to take you back to Ujjayini with him. You'll be honoured by the royal court.'

> *Matul stops again.*

Hearing this, his lordship paused. Pausing, he looked at me with fire in his eyes. 'I'm not here to be bought and sold with royal coin.' He said this as though the coins of the royal treasury were consumed by longing for him, and then he left. . . . I fell into a moral predicament: should I pursue his lordship, begging and pleading, or should I look after my guests? Then I came here, after telling this Nikshep to stay with the Acharya—and now, like a wheel that has spun off its axle, he has come careening after me.

NIKSHEP: But, Matul, I've just come to inform you that . . .

MATUL: And I thank you for keeping me informed. Well done! The guests are sitting over there without a host, and you've come all the way here to inform me! . . . And, now, just do me this one favour—wherever that crown jewel of the tribe of poets may be, please find him and bring him back.

> *Matul moves towards the exit.*

My sense of duty tells me that I should find whatever way I can to present him before the Acharya. . . . And my brain tells me that, wherever I find him, I should seize him then and there by the tuft of his poetic hair, and . . .

Matul exits. [see pp. 105–07]

Matul is on stage with three other characters on this occasion, and he addresses each of them, in turn, in the rapid-fire mode that is typical of such comic scenes. He speaks to each of his interlocutors, either directly or indirectly, on three distinct subjects: he addresses the passage as a whole to Ambika, responding to an earlier comment by her with 'you talk about his public relations' at the beginning of this quotation; he directs his interjection, 'No, I don't want a seat', specifically at Mallika, while also referring to Ambika's gesture of courtesy; and, towards the end of the quotation, he speaks to Nikshep, initially in the third person but then, after a quick shift, in the second person, about the logistics of their situation. A socialized village elder, Matul employs different tones of voice to address his fellow characters: he talks to Ambika as an equal in age and status and as a lifelong friend, but also as a visitor of the moment, bound by courtesy; he addresses Mallika in passing, but as a family 'familiar', a benevolent avuncular presence; and he speaks to Nikshep as a superior in age and status who, in a frenetic state, is free to berate his negligent and inexperienced helpmate.

In Hindi, Matul modulates his tone rather precisely for these interlocutors, even as he spirals into a 'scatterbrained' overreaction. But he also has two other pressing concerns, pushing him simultaneously in other directions—the acharya from Ujjayini, to whom he must attend, and Kalidas himself, the ward for whom he feels responsible, and whose irresponsible response has thrown him into a tizzy in the first place. For his comments on the acharya, Matul uses a tone of deference, the kind reserved for a social superior who must not be slighted; but, for his description and narration of Kalidas, he opts for mock deference and sarcasm, even performing an entire satirical impression—in the style of stand-up comedy—of the poet and their (to him) infuriating confrontation. Thus, in barely eighteen sentences, some of them quite short and all of them brilliantly conversational, Rakesh makes Matul take on five diverse themes, employ five divergent styles or tones, and deal with three disparate respondents, all of them rolled into one circumambient discourse—the babble of a good-natured uncle who is a bit of an unwitting buffoon and, like T.S. Eliot's Polonius in 'The Love Song of J. Alfred Prufrock', also a bit of an 'officious fool'. The manifold layering of the scene becomes evident when we notice that Matul's metaphor for Nikshep, towards the end, is also Rakesh's metaphor for Matul and this scene, which together are 'like a wheel that has spun off its axle' and come careening at us, outside the text and the performance space. To do justice on a relatively large scale to a passage of this sort, the translation has to be 'literal' and 'literary' in equal measure on multiple levels, keeping the syntax constantly in focus.

The other vignette, which exemplifies complexity on a small scale, comes from the (unmarked) second scene in Act Three, where Mallika has just heard that Kalidas has relinquished his office at the royal court—initially that of court poet, but subsequently elevated to that of royal son-in-law and governor of the imperial province of Kashmir. Speaking aloud to herself while alone on stage, as the audience eavesdrops on her but the play's other characters cannot, she says (addressing the absent Kalidas as 'you'):

> I go to the mountain peak even now and look at the garlands of clouds, just as before. I read lines from *A Gathering of Seasons* and *The Cloud-Messenger*, just as before. I haven't allowed the womb of my emotion to become barren. But can you measure the pain of my deprivation?
>
>> *She sits down on the floor, with her elbows on the seat, and picks up the blank book.*
>
> No, you can't measure it. You once wrote that a single flaw hides itself in a crowd of virtues, just as the moon's blemish hides itself in a multitude of rays—but destitution can't hide itself. It can't hide itself even in a hundred good qualities. Not only can it not hide, it overshadows a hundred good qualities—destroys them, one by one.
>
>> *As she speaks, she grows more deeply introspective.*
>
> But I endured all this. Because, even as I was breaking, I felt that you were making yourself. Because I saw myself, not in my own self, but in you. . . .
>
>> *Lightning flashes and the sound of thunder can be heard.*
>> [see pp. 169]

In Hindi, we witness this moment—textually, in the mind's eye and, theatrically, in the mise en scène—as a 'spontaneous overflow of powerful feelings', but Mallika's expressiveness is achieved with an intricately fabricated trope embedded in one sentence in the middle: 'You once wrote that a single flaw hides itself in a crowd of virtues, just as the moon's blemish hides itself in a multitude of rays—but destitution can't hide itself.' The first part of Mallika's quotation from Kalidas's poetry—'a single flaw hides itself in a crowd of virtues'—is an antiparallel metonymy; in the second part, it is equated to a second metonymy of the same kind, though the internal logic is different.[8] According to Aristotle's fourth criterion for metaphorical identification between two entities (identification by analogy), this equation is a metaphor and not a simile, so the line that Mallika recalls and quotes is an extended metonymous metaphor.[9] Complicated as this figure already is, Rakesh expands it further with Mallika's crucial qualification, that 'destitution can't hide itself'. The two-part metonymous metaphor thus protracts into another antiparallelism, with a 'broken metonym' at its end, in which 'destitution' now is a tenor without an imaginable vehicle. Mallika's antithetical threefold analogy, however, is so apt and elegant that its figural logic makes her self-reflection irrefutable, raising emotion to *pathos*, in the Greek sense of the term.[10] If we were to substitute it with a declarative sentence, stripped of all the machinery of metaphor, the effect on Rakesh's atmospheric stage simply would not be the same. The consequence is that our translation is obliged to follow his footwork as nimbly as possible, so that Mallika's words can still 'trip off her tongue' with the greatest aesthetic ease, without disturbing the illusion that she is 'speaking from the heart'. In other words, the literalism of our translation has to be integrated completely and invisibly with Rakesh's 'artless art'.

The text of *Ashadh ka ek din* that we have rendered appears in *Mohan rakesh ke sampurna natak* (The Complete Plays of Mohan Rakesh, 1993), edited by Nemichandra Jain, which has been the standard source of Rakesh's collected full-length plays in Hindi for over two decades. A.K. Ramanujan's practice as a translator also reminds us that literary translations have a double obligation, and hence involve a double movement: to carry an unfamiliar text from one language into another, across the gulf that separates them; and, at the same time, to carry the reader of the second language into the first, across the same gulf but in the opposite direction. Commentary thus becomes an indispensable supplement in the translator's effort to domesticate a literary work in an environment that is foreign to it, transporting the reader towards the territory of the original, which is alien to him or her.[11] We have framed our translation of *Ashadh* with an array of materials that will help general readers and theatre professionals, students and teachers, as well as scholars and specialists to make their figurative way to Rakesh's country.

Quite apart from our concerns with craft and representation—the dialectic of literalism and literariness— our most important practical objective with this translation has been its potential for performance in English on the cosmopolitan stage. As Rakesh notes in his preface to the second edition of *Ashadh* in September 1958, his own primary criterion for the success of drama is its performability, and he views performance as the telos (design, purpose, or end) built into the mechanics of a play.[12] In spite of his vision and desire, *Ashadh* entered the sphere of print several months before it could reach the Hindi stage; the delay, however, may have been a blessing in disguise for the intersection—still emerging in India at the time—of dramatic production in multiple languages and multilingual theatrical practice in postcolonial space. But once Indian theatre groups began to circumnavigate the play's possibilities on the proscenium and in environmental arenas, its staging quickly became a 'legendary' experience, not only for directors and actors but also for set engineers, costume designers, make-up artists, and sound and lighting technicians. As the Introduction observes, over the past five decades, actors in particular—especially stage actresses, whose careers were defined by the role of Mallika—have found that this play has an unusual power to expand their repertoires, to deepen their emotional reach, and even to affect their private lives offstage. Much of our coordinated effort with the translation has been to polish it as a versatile performance vehicle, a rare contemporary example of drama that uses classical skill on a classical scale to fuse telling and showing, diegesis and mimesis, words and action. We therefore hope that directors, dramaturges, actors, and production designers will explore it with art and imagination, and 'make it new' for themselves, for the theatre, and for audiences everywhere.

One Day in
the Season
of Rain

Dramatis Personae

AMBIKA	an old woman in the village
MALLIKA	her daughter
KALIDAS	a poet
DANTUL	a courtier
MATUL	the poet's uncle
NIKSHEP	a man from the village
VILOM	a man from the village
RANGINI	a woman from the city
SANGINI	a woman from the city
ANUSVAR	an official
ANUNASIK	an official
PRIYANGUMANJARI	a princess—the poet's wife

Act One

Before the curtain rises, soft sounds of thunder and rain, which continue for a few moments after, then gradually fade away.

The curtain rises slowly.

An ordinary room. The walls are made of wood, but their lower portion is plastered with smooth clay. Hindu swastika symbols are painted here and there in vermilion. The front door opens into a dark entranceway. On either side of the doorway are small niches containing little unlit clay lamps. A door upstage left leads to a second room. When this door is open, only one corner of a simple bed is visible. Both doors are also plastered with clay, and are decorated with outlines of lotuses and conch shells in vermilion and deep yellow. Upstage right is a large lattice window through which lightning is occasionally visible.

On one side of the room is a small wood-burning clay stove. Clay and brass pots and pans are arranged neatly around it. On the other side, at some distance from the lattice window, are three or four large clay jars discoloured by soot and moss. Their mouths are covered with reed mats kept in place with stone weights. Next to the lattice window is a wooden seat with a tiger skin draped over it. Near the stove are two low square stools.

Ambika sits on one of the square stools, husking grain in a reed winnowing pan. She looks towards the window once, sighs deeply, and again busies herself with the winnowing.

The front door opens and Mallika enters, shivering and hugging herself in wet clothes. Ambika remains busy, with her eyes lowered. Mallika pauses for a moment, then approaches her.

MALLIKA: The first day of the season of rain, and such rain, Ma. Such torrents of rain. Even the most distant foothills were drenched. And me, too. See how wet I am, Ma!

> *Ambika looks her up and down once, and gets busy again. Mallika kneels down and rests her head on Ambika's shoulder.*

I went out thinking I'd watch the flight of cranes coming in from the south, and now, look, all my clothes are soaking wet.

> *She kisses her mother's hair and stands up, shivering with cold.*

Where are my dry clothes, Ma? If I stand here like this, I'll freeze. . . . Why aren't you saying anything?

> *Ambika looks at her angrily.*

AMBIKA: The dry clothes are on the bed inside.

MALLIKA: You've already put them out?

> *She goes towards the inner room.*

You knew I'd get wet. And I knew you'd be worried. But, Ma . . .

Near the door she turns and looks at Ambika.

. . . I'm not at all sorry about getting wet. If I hadn't gotten wet, I'd have been deprived of something today.

She leans against the door frame.

Smoky clouds had gathered all around. I knew it was going to rain. Yet I kept going down and down the trail, into the valley. At one point, the wind even blew away my wrap. Then it began to drizzle.

Her gaze meets Ambika's.

Let me change, then I'll come and tell you. That was an amazing experience, Ma—really amazing.

Mallika goes inside. Ambika gets up and puts the winnowed grain into one of the large jars, and takes out fresh grain from another. Mallika's words continue to be heard from the inner room. The audience also catches a glimpse of her every now and then.

Tender and moist like the blue lotus, gentle as a breeze, and picturesque as a dream! I wanted to fill myself with the experience, and close my eyes. . . . Even my body's being wrung out, Ma! How much water have my clothes soaked in! Oh! After the bite of cold, this touch of warmth!

She begins to hum.

[*Song*] The water lily that is blue,
       Blue without a blemish,
           Is vain about its eminence . . .

Where shall I put the wet clothes, Ma? Shall I leave them here?

[*Song*] The mildest movements stir,
Stir the gentle breeze,
In all its gentleness . . .

Travellers, in distress
Without their homely women,
Are vexed and perplexed . . .

She returns to the front room.

I'll never forget those moments today, Ma. I've never witnessed such beauty before. As though that beauty were intangible—yet substantial. I could touch it, see it, drink it in. In that instant I understood what turns feeling into poetry. For the first time in my life I understood why someone would get lost in a train of clouds caressing the mountain peaks, why someone would be so enchanted by images appearing and disappearing in the sky, instead of being absorbed in his own body and mind . . . What's the matter, Ma? Why are you so quiet?

AMBIKA: You can see I'm working.

MALLIKA: Well, you're working all the while. But you aren't quiet like this all the time.

She comes and sits near Ambika, who continues to winnow the grain in silence. Mallika takes the winnowing pan from her hand.

I won't let you work. . . . Talk to me.

AMBIKA: What do you want me to say?

MALLIKA: Say anything. Scold me for coming back soaked. Or tell me that you're tired, so I should husk the rest of the grain. Or say that you were home alone and didn't like it.

AMBIKA: I like everything.

Ambika takes the winnowing pan from Mallika.

And when am I not alone at home? Am I not alone even when you're here?

MALLIKA: I'm not going to let you work any more.

She takes back the winnowing pan from Ambika's hand, and puts it down near the large jars.

You're alone even when I'm home? . . . Sometimes you reproach me for getting in the way of your work when I stay at home. And sometimes you say . . .

She puts her arms around Ambika's neck from behind.

Tell me, why are you so sombre?

AMBIKA: I've boiled the milk. Add some sugar and drink it.

MALLIKA: No, answer me first.

AMBIKA: And go rest on the bed for a little while. I still have to . . .

MALLIKA: No, Ma, I don't want to rest. Why should I rest when I'm not tired? Within me, I can still feel the thrilling sensation of the raindrops falling on my skin. Every fibre of my being is still tingling. Why don't you answer me? If you keep doing this, I won't talk to you, either.

*Saying nothing, Ambika wipes her eyes with the end
of her sari. She then pushes Mallika away from behind
herself, and makes her sit down on one of the nearer
square stools. Mallika looks at Ambika silently for a
moment.*

What's happened, Ma? Why are you crying?

AMBIKA: Nothing, Mallika! Sometimes one feels sad for no
reason.

MALLIKA: One feels sad for no reason. But one doesn't just sit
and cry. . . . If you don't tell me what's wrong, Ma, you'll
be forsworn.

*Some noises and the sound of horses' hooves are heard
in the distance. Ambika rises and goes to the window.
Mallika remains seated for a moment, then she, too,
walks to the window and looks out. The sound of
hooves approaches and then recedes.*

Who are these people, Ma?

AMBIKA: They're probably royal court officials.

MALLIKA: What are they doing here?

AMBIKA: Who knows what they're doing! . . . Every few years
these characters turn up in our village. And, whenever they
appear, there's some calamity or other. Sometimes they
bring news of a war, sometimes of an epidemic.

She takes a deep breath.

When your father died in the last plague, I'd seen the same
figures here.

Mallika shudders from head to toe.

MALLIKA: But why have these people come here today?

AMBIKA: Who knows why they've come.

Ambika tries to pick up the winnowing pan again, but Mallika grabs her arm and stops her.

MALLIKA: Ma, you haven't told me what's wrong.

Ambika stares at her for a moment. Mallika lowers her eyes.

AMBIKA: Agnimitra has come back today.

Ambika picks up the winnowing pan and goes back to her stool. Mallika remains standing at the window.

MALLIKA: He has come back? From where?

AMBIKA: From where I sent him.

MALLIKA: You sent him?

Her lips begin to quiver. She advances towards Ambika.

But I'd told you there was no need to send Agnimitra anywhere.

Gradually her voice grows more agitated.

You know I don't want to get married, then why do you keep trying? Do you think I just rant and rave pointlessly?

Ambika takes up fistfuls of grain, rubs it between her palms, and lets it drop into the winnowing pan.

AMBIKA: I can see that things are turning out exactly as you wanted. Agnimitra has brought back the message that the people to whom I'd sent him aren't interested in this match. They say . . .

MALLIKA: What do they say? What right do they have to say anything at all? Mallika's life is her own property. If she wants to destroy it, then who has the right to criticize her?

AMBIKA: When have I said that I have the right?

Mallika turns her head sharply and tries to suppress her agitation.

MALLIKA: I'm not talking about your rights.

AMBIKA: You may not say it, but I'm saying it. Today your life is your own property. I have no rights over you.

Mallika sits down on the other square stool and places her hand on Ambika's shoulder.

MALLIKA: Why do you talk like this? . . . Why don't you try to understand me?

Ambika removes Mallika's hand from her shoulder.

AMBIKA: I know that, today, even you don't have any rights over yourself. But I can't bear such a huge transgression.

Mallika crosses her arms over her knees and rests her head on them.

MALLIKA: Ma, I know there's unpleasant talk. I also understand your unhappiness. And yet I don't feel guilty. I've followed an impulse and chosen one emotion out of many. For me, that one bond is greater than all other bonds. I'm really in love with my emotion—which is pure, tender, eternal.

Ambika's face becomes distorted.

AMBIKA: And I feel repelled by such an emotion. 'Pure, tender, eternal!' *Hunh!*

MALLIKA: Ma, why don't you trust me?

AMBIKA: What you call emotion is only duplicity and self-deception. 'I've followed an impulse and chosen one emotion!' . . . I ask you, what does it mean to choose emotion on an impulse? How does that fulfil the necessities of life? . . . 'Chosen one emotion on an impulse!' *Hunh!*

Mallika stares at the ceiling for a moment.

MALLIKA: The gross necessities of life aren't everything, Ma. There's so much else besides them.

Ambika begins to winnow the grain again.

AMBIKA: Maybe there is—I don't know.

Mallika looks at Ambika for a few moments.

MALLIKA: The truth is, Ma, like other people in the village, you too look at him with suspicion and revulsion.

AMBIKA: The other people in the village don't know him as well as I do.

For a moment they stare at each other.

I detest him.

Mallika's face becomes marked with anguish, helplessness, and strong emotion.

MALLIKA: Ma!

AMBIKA: What do other people have to do with him? But I do. His influence is destroying my home.

Kalidas's voice can be heard from the direction of the entranceway. The lines on Ambika's brow deepen. She stands up with the winnowing pan. She looks towards the entrance for a moment, then walks towards the inner room.

MALLIKA: Wait, Ma, why're you leaving?

AMBIKA: A mother's life is action, not emotion. She has a lot to do around the house.

Ambika leaves. Kalidas enters, carrying a fawn in his arms and soothing it. Blood drips from the fawn's body.

KALIDAS: We'll live, little fawn, won't we? We won't give up our life just for being wounded by an arrow. So what if our body's tender. We can endure pain. If an arrow can take life, then a hand's gentle touch can also give life. We'll find new life. We'll rest on some soft blankets. Our limbs will be massaged with oil. Tomorrow we'll roam in the forest again. Feed on succulent grass. Won't we?

Mallika gathers herself and goes towards the door.

MALLIKA: This wounded fawn . . . what kind of person here would have wounded it? Is it that, as in the south, here too . . . ?

KALIDAS: I've noticed many new presences in our rural province today.

He moves towards the window seat and sits down on it.

Some officials from the royal court have come to the village.

He hugs the fawn to his chest and starts soothing it.

KALIDAS: Will we go to sleep now? Yes, if we sleep for a little while, our pain will go away. But, before that, we've to drink some milk. . . . Mallika, if you have some milk, get it in a bowl.

MALLIKA: Ma has boiled the milk. I'll go see.

> *She goes to the clay stove and starts looking among the pots and pans around it.*

Just a little while ago we saw two or three royal officials passing by on horseback. Ma says that whenever these people appear, there's some calamity or other. After the exhilaration of the rain . . . I found all this very strange.

> *She picks up the pot of milk and begins to pour some into a bowl.*

Ma's very upset today.

> *Kalidas begins to rock the fawn in his arms.*

KALIDAS: We're happier than before. Our pain's slowly receding. We're getting better. . . . I don't understand how he could shoot an arrow at this body that's soft as cotton. It came bounding into my lap. I said, 'I'll take you where you'll find eyes like your mother's, and love like hers, too.'

> *He looks at Mallika. She comes up to him with the milk.*

MALLIKA: Really, Ma's very upset today. She must have realized that I was with you in the rain—otherwise I wouldn't have come back soaking wet. Ma's always so worried about scandal.

KALIDAS: Let me hold the milk, and you take the fawn in your arms.

> *He takes the bowl from Mallika's hand. She takes the*
> *fawn in her arms and brings its mouth close to the*
> *milk. Kalidas brings the bowl even closer.*

KALIDAS: We won't drink the milk? No—we aren't going to be so obstinate! We'll certainly drink the milk.

> *The courtier Dantul enters and pauses near the door.*
> *He watches them for a moment. Kalidas holds the milk*
> *to the fawn's mouth.*

Yes, like this . . . like this.

> *Dantul advances into the room and draws close to*
> *them.*

DANTUL: You want to give it milk and make its flesh even more tender?

> *Kalidas and Mallika look at him, startled. Mallika*
> *retreats a little with the fawn. Kalidas places the bowl*
> *of milk on the seat next to himself.*

KALIDAS: So far as I know, we aren't acquainted—how did you dare to enter a home where you're a stranger?

> *Dantul looks once at Mallika, then at Kalidas.*

DANTUL: What a coincidence—I wanted to ask you exactly the same kind of question! We've never been acquainted, but you had no scruples about carrying away a deer brought down by my arrow. Luckily, there's a trail of blood leading to this door—otherwise, would I have been able to track you down on this dark, overcast day?

KALIDAS: I can see that you're not a native of this region.

Dantul laughs sarcastically.

DANTUL: I applaud your insight! My appearance itself is an indication that I don't belong to this place.

KALIDAS: I'm not saying this because of your appearance.

DANTUL: After looking at the lines on my brow, then? It seems that, besides robbery, you also practise clairvoyance.

Mallika advances a little, looking as though she is hurt.

MALLIKA: Don't you feel any shame in casting such aspersions?

DANTUL: Forgive me, lady. But this fawn you're carrying in your arms has been wounded by my arrow. So it's my property. You'll return my property to me, won't you?

KALIDAS: In this province, there's no hunting of deer, sir. You're an outsider, so it's enough that we don't treat you as a criminal for this act.

DANTUL: So villagers will sit in judgement on a courtier for a crime! My rustic friend, do you even know the meaning of crime and justice?

KALIDAS: It's surprising to learn that words and meanings are the property of courtiers.

DANTUL: You seem to be a smart fellow. Yet you don't know that the rights of courtiers extend far and wide. I'm getting late. Give me this fawn.

KALIDAS: This fawn is the property of this mountain region, sir. And we, the inhabitants of this region, are its kinsmen.

You're making a mistake if you think that we'll hand it over to you. . . . Mallika, take it inside and lay it down on the bed or on a blanket. . . .

Ambika emerges suddenly from the interior.

AMBIKA: The beds and blankets in this house aren't meant for fawns.

MALLIKA: You can see, Ma . . . !

AMBIKA: Yes, I can see. That's why I'm speaking out. The beds and blankets are for people, not for animals.

KALIDAS: Give me the fawn, Mallika!

He puts the bowl of milk down on the floor and advances to take the fawn in his arms.

The cushion of my arms will be enough for it. I'll take it home with me.

He walks towards the door.

DANTUL: And Dantul the courtier will simply watch you taking it away!

KALIDAS: That depends on the courtier's preference.

He walks to the entrance without glancing at Dantul.

DANTUL: Perhaps it will be necessary to acquaint you with what the likes and dislikes of a courtier are.

Kalidas leaves. Only his response is heard offstage.

KALIDAS: Perhaps.

DANTUL: Perhaps?

He wants to go after Kalidas, with his hand on his sword. Mallika moves quickly to stand between Dantul and the door.

MALLIKA: Stop, sir! Don't insist on taking the fawn. For you it's a question of your right, for him it's a question of compassion—though unarmed, Kalidas won't think twice about your weapon.

DANTUL: Kalidas? . . . You mean to say that the man with whom I was arguing about the fawn is the poet Kalidas?

MALLIKA: Yes—yes. But how do you know that Kalidas is a poet?

DANTUL: How do I know! Every member of Ujjayini's royal court knows of the poet Kalidas, the author of the poem *A Gathering of Seasons*.

MALLIKA: Every member of Ujjayini's royal court knows of him?

DANTUL: The emperor himself has read *A Gathering of Seasons* and praised it. That's why the court now wants to honour its author, and offer him the position of court poet. That's precisely why Acharya Vararuchi has come here from Ujjayini.

On hearing this, Mallika seems to freeze with astonishment.

MALLIKA: The court wants to honour him? Offer him the position of court poet . . . ?

DANTUL: I regret that my conduct with him was uncivil. I should go and apologize to him.

He leaves. Mallika remains standing like that for a few moments. Then suddenly she seems to become conscious again. In the meantime, Ambika picks up the bowl of milk and puts it in a corner. She looks at the pot of milk, pours the rest of the milk into a smaller tumbler, adds some sugar, and stirs it. Her hands are trembling, as though she is deeply agitated. Biting her lower lip, Mallika runs up to her.

MALLIKA: Did you hear, Ma? The royal court wants to offer him the position of court poet.

Ambika somehow holds on to the tumbler of milk about to fall from her hands.

AMBIKA: I've spread the wet clothes out to dry. There's a little milk left, and I've added sugar to it.

MALLIKA: Ma, didn't you hear what the courtier was saying?

AMBIKA: Drink your milk. I hope nobody else needs to be welcomed here now.

MALLIKA: Welcomed? . . . I'd like to be able to welcome the whole world into this home today.

She takes the tumbler from Ambika's hand.

Shall I bathe you in this milk, Ma?

She raises the tumbler. Ambika snatches it from her hand.

AMBIKA: I've done enough bathing in milk already.

MALLIKA: How heartless you are, Ma! Didn't you hear that the court's honouring him? Even then, you . . .

AMBIKA: Drink your milk. And if you aren't tempted to get wet in the rain again, I'll prepare your bed for the night. . . Let me remain heartless, as I am.

Mallika puts her arms around Ambika's neck.

MALLIKA: No, you aren't heartless. When did I say you're heartless?

AMBIKA: No, you didn't say it. Drink your milk.

Mallika takes the tumbler from her hand, finishes the milk in a single gulp, and puts it down in a corner. Then she pulls Ambika by the hand, makes her sit down, and lies down with her head in Ambika's lap.

MALLIKA: Ma, can you imagine how happy I am today?

AMBIKA: I don't have the strength to think about anything. Now let me get up, I have lots of work to do.

She tries to get up, but Mallika holds her down.

MALLIKA: No, don't get up. Just sit like this. . . . The court's honouring him, Ma! He'll hold the position of court poet . . .

Suddenly she leaves Ambika's lap and sits up.

. . . he, whom the people close to him have never tried to understand, to this day. Who has only been attacked and disgraced inside and outside his home . . . Surely, you can now believe, Ma, that my emotion isn't baseless.

Ambika stands up.

AMBIKA: I've already told you that my power to think and understand is gone.

MALLIKA: Why, Ma? Why are you so prejudiced? Why can't you think of him with generosity?

AMBIKA: I'm past the stage at which one can live with one's eyes shut to reality.

She moves towards the interior. Mallika stands up.

MALLIKA: And your realistic vision can see nothing but flaws?

Ambika turns and stares at her for a moment.

AMBIKA: Where there's a flaw, my vision certainly sees a flaw.

MALLIKA: What flaw do you see in him?

AMBIKA: That man is completely self-centred. He has no attachments to anyone other than himself in the whole world.

MALLIKA: Only because he doesn't tend to his uncle Matul's cows, and remains lost in the clouds?

AMBIKA: I'm not concerned with Matul and his cows. I'm looking only at my own home when I say this.

MALLIKA: Sit down, Ma!

She grabs Ambika by the hand and takes her to the window seat.

I want to understand what you're saying.

AMBIKA: I, too, want you to understand this today. . . . You say your bond with him is one of emotion. What's that emotion?

MALLIKA: I don't give it any name.

She sits down at Ambika's feet.

AMBIKA: But people do give it a name. . . . If he really has an emotional bond with you, then why doesn't he want to marry you?

MALLIKA: You've always been ungenerous towards him, Ma. You know the ironies of circumstance in which his life has been spent. What his condition has been in Matul's home. In that life of deprivation, without resources, how could marriage even be imagined?

AMBIKA: And now, when his life will no longer be deprived and lacking in resources?

Mallika falls silent for a few moments and stares at her feet.

However great a reason deprivation is for avoiding commitment, the end of deprivation becomes an even greater reason for refusing to commit.

MALLIKA: This is Vilom's language, not yours.

AMBIKA: I understand his kind of man very well. His only connection with you is that you're a receptacle and a refuge through which he can love himself, be proud of himself. But aren't you a flesh-and-blood person? Don't you—and doesn't he—have any obligation towards you? Tomorrow, when your mother will no longer be physically present, and there will be no arrangement in the house for even one proper meal a day, how will you answer the question confronting you? Will your emotion be able to resolve that question? Tell me again that this is Vilom's language, not mine.

*Mallika sits silently for a few moments, with her head
bowed. Then she looks at Ambika.*

MALLIKA: Ma, life has somehow managed to pass so far. What's
yet to come will also pass. But today, when his life's
taking a new direction, I don't want to stand before him,
proclaiming my self-interest.

Matul's voice is heard offstage.

MATUL: Ambika! . . . Ambika! Are you home, or aren't you?

*Ambika and Mallika look towards the entranceway.
Matul enters in a dishevelled state.*

Indeed, you're home! I'm going to announce to the entire
village that I have no connection whatever with this
creature who bears the name of Kalidas.

MALLIKA: What has happened, Arya Matul?

MATUL: I raised him, I nurtured him. All for this day—so that
he could betray his clan like this?

MALLIKA: But what we've heard is that he's being honoured
by the royal court. Some senior scholar has come from
Ujjayini.

MATUL: That's exactly what I'm saying. Some scholar has come
from Ujjayini.

MALLIKA: But you were just saying. . . .

MATUL: I'm saying it right. The scholar wants to take Kalidas
with him to Ujjayini right away, tomorrow.

MALLIKA: But . . .

MATUL: He has come with two chariots, two charioteers, and four mounted guards. Didn't I always tell you, Ambika, that the son of the son of the daughter of the founding father of our clan fought for the Gupta empire against the Shaka invaders?

AMBIKA: You were talking about your sister's son.

MATUL: I'm still talking about him. You should understand that, in one respect, the court's honouring our entire clan. And this glorious descendent of our clan says, 'I don't want this honour . . .'

Mallika stands up abruptly.

'I'm not here to be bought and sold with royal coin,' he says.

*Matul begins to pace up and down the room excitedly.
Mallika stands oblivious for a few moments.*

MALLIKA: He doesn't want to accept the court's honour?

MATUL: I can't understand how buying and selling comes into this business. If you're given an honour, accept it. Otherwise, what's poetry worth?

MALLIKA: Poetry has some value, Arya Matul, that's why the honour also has value. . . . I can understand where this honour pricks his conscience.

Lost in thought, Ambika begins to twist the end of her sari in her fingers.

AMBIKA: I assure you, Matul, that he'll definitely go to Ujjayini.

Matul continues to pace.

MATUL: He'll definitely go! These people of course are his devotees who'll sing his praises and carry him away!

AMBIKA: When a person receives an honour, the indifference he expresses towards it increases his importance. You should be happy that your sister's son is well versed in public relations, too.

Matul stops suddenly.

MATUL: If this is public relations, then I'll have to say that public relations and pinhead relations amount to the same thing.

He resumes pacing.

When a person offers something—whether wealth or honour—he can also change his mind—and when the mind changes, it changes.

He stops again.

You think about it—the emperor can even take offence that an ordinary poet has turned down his honour.

Nikshep enters.

NIKSHEP: Matul, you're still here, while the Acharya's waiting for you over there.

MATUL: And what are you doing here, Nikshep? Didn't I tell you to stay with the Acharya until I got back?

NIKSHEP: But you also told me to inform you as soon as the Acharya had finished resting.

MATUL: Yes, I said this. But I also said that. This you could understand, but that you couldn't?

NIKSHEP: But, Matul . . .

MATUL: But what? Is Matul a fool? Tell me, do you think I'm a fool?

NIKSHEP: No, Matul . . .

MATUL: If I'm not a fool, then you're a fool, for sure. . . . What has the Acharya said?

NIKSHEP: He has said that he wants to tour this entire village region with you . . .

An expression of pride appears on Matul's face.

. . . the region that gave birth to Kalidas's poetry.

Matul's expression changes to one of revulsion.

MATUL: Kalidas's poetry!

He starts pacing again.

God knows what special qualities such a great scholar sees in his poetry!

He pauses and looks at Ambika.

This man has no sense of even ordinary conduct with people, and you talk about his public relations. . . . His lordship was coming home with a fawn in his arms. Luckily, I spotted him just outside the house. I pleaded with him: 'O master of the tribe of poets, this is not the time to enter our home in such a state. A great scholar has come for you from Ujjayini, and is waiting for you.' As soon as he heard this, his lordship turned away. As though he'd seen a snake in his path.

> *Mallika sits down near Ambika on the window seat.*
> *Matul resumes pacing.*

AMBIKA: Mallika, bring Matul a seat from the inner room.

> *Mallika begins to rise, but Matul stops her.*

MATUL: No, I don't want a seat. The Acharya's waiting for me.

> *Nikshep looks at Ambika and smiles. Matul walks up*
> *to the end of the room and turns back.*

I said to him, 'O poet supreme, the Acharya's here to take you back to Ujjayini with him. You'll be honoured by the royal court.'

> *Matul stops again.*

Hearing this, his lordship paused. Pausing, he looked at me with fire in his eyes. 'I'm not here to be bought and sold with royal coin.' He said this as though the coins of the royal treasury were consumed by longing for him, and then he left. . . . I fell into a moral predicament: should I pursue his lordship, begging and pleading, or should I look after my guests? Then I came here, after telling this Nikshep to stay with the Acharya—and now, like a wheel that has spun off its axle, he has come careening after me.

NIKSHEP: But, Matul, I've just come to inform you that . . .

MATUL: And I thank you for keeping me informed. Well done! The guests are sitting over there without a host, and you've come all the way here to inform me! . . . And, now, just do me this one favour—wherever that crown jewel of the tribe of poets may be, please find him and bring him back.

Matul moves towards the exit.

My sense of duty tells me that I should find whatever way I can to present him before the Acharya. . . . And my brain tells me that, wherever I find him, I should seize him then and there by the tuft of his poetic hair, and . . .

Matul exits.

NIKSHEP: Matul's third eye is always open.

MALLIKA: But where's Kalidas right now?

NIKSHEP: Kalidas is at the temple of the goddess Jagdamba at this moment.

MALLIKA: Have you seen him?

NIKSHEP: I've seen him.

MALLIKA: But you didn't tell Matul?

NIKSHEP: I didn't want Matul to go there straight away.

MALLIKA: Why? You, too, don't want Kalidas to . . . ?

NIKSHEP: I definitely want Kalidas to go to Ujjayini. That's why I didn't think it would be appropriate for Matul to go to him at this time. . . . Matul gets so much pleasure from listening to the words coming out of his mouth that he just goes on talking, and doesn't want to understand the situation around him. . . . Kalidas is insisting that until the guests from Ujjayini have left, he'll stay on in Jagdamba's temple and not return home.

AMBIKA: What far-sightedness!

NIKSHEP: Far-sightedness?

AMBIKA: Of course, it's far-sightedness.

NIKSHEP: Where's the far-sightedness in this, Ambika!

Ambika gives Nikshep a sharp look.

AMBIKA: The court wants to honour the poet. Indifferent to the honour, the poet's lost in meditation at Jagdamba's temple. The court's representatives come to the temple and supplicate the poet. The poet opens his eyes very slowly . . . Isn't it far-sighted to create such a big drama?

NIKSHEP: Kalidas isn't creating a drama, Ambika! I'm convinced that courtly honours don't hold any attraction for him. He really doesn't want to leave this mountain region.

Ambika rises from her seat and goes towards the pots and pans near the stove.

AMBIKA: Doesn't want to leave! . . . *Hunh!*

She takes a platter to one of the jars and begins to take out fistfuls of rice grain.

NIKSHEP: No one's persuasion—neither Matul's nor anyone else's—can overcome his obstinacy.

He gives Mallika a meaningful look. She lowers her eyes.

There's only one person at whose request he could possibly give up his stubbornness.

Ambika sizes up Nikshep's meaningful look and then looks at Mallika.

AMBIKA: No one in our house is concerned at all whether he gives up his obstinacy or not.

Ambika takes the platter to the stove and, with her back to the other two, tries to busy herself.

NIKSHEP: In his sensitivity, Kalidas is forgetting that he'll lose a great deal by disregarding this opportunity. Ability moulds only one quarter of one's personality—fame and recognition complete the rest. Kalidas should definitely go to the royal capital.

Ambika tries to appear busy but fails.

AMBIKA: So what's impeding him?

NIKSHEP: I've sensed that somewhere, at the root of his obstinacy, there's a streak of profound bitterness.

MALLIKA: I know where that streak lies. . . . He's had a confrontation with a courtier a little while ago.

NIKSHEP: Only you can dispel that bitterness, Mallika! Opportunity doesn't wait for anybody. If Kalidas doesn't leave this place, the court won't lose anything. The office of court poet won't remain vacant. But, for the rest of his life, Kalidas will remain what he is today—a local poet! Even the people who're praising *A Gathering of Seasons* today will forget him in a short while.

Mallika, seemingly lost in thought, stands up abruptly.

MALLIKA: No, he mustn't disparage this honour. This is a tribute to his poetic self. He shouldn't deprive that self of its rights. Come, I'll go with you to Jagdamba's temple.

Ambika gets up suddenly.

AMBIKA: Mallika!

Mallika gives Ambika a steady look.

MALLIKA: Ma!

AMBIKA: Will I have to say in front of an outsider that I'm not in favour of your going there at this time?

NIKSHEP: Nikshep is not an outsider, Ambika!

MALLIKA: This is a crucial moment, Ma! I really must go there right now. Come, Arya Nikshep.

> *Mallika exits, without glancing at Ambika. A wave of anger crosses Ambika's face, and changes into an expression of defeat. Nikshep stands still for a moment, observing Ambika's emotions.*

NIKSHEP: Please forgive me, Ambika.

> *He follows Mallika. Ambika remains standing for a few moments with her eyes closed. Then she stares at the household objects around her one by one, and, as though broken, sits down on a stool and begins to rub the rice grains lying on the platter between her palms. Her eyes brim over with tears, which she wipes with the end of her sari. The lights dim. A choked sound escapes her lips.*

AMBIKA: Emotion! . . . Oh!

> *She covers her face with the end of her sari. The lights dim further. Just then the glow of a wooden torch appears in the darkness of the entranceway. Vilom enters with a torch in his hands. At the sight of Ambika sitting like this, he pauses momentarily. Then he draws close to her.*

VILOM: The gathered clouds have cast an untimely darkness today, Ambika—or did you lose track of time?

*Ambika raises her head from her sari. In the torchlight,
her face looks furrowed and her eyes appear sunken.*

I'm surprised that you haven't lit the lamps as yet.

AMBIKA: Vilom! . . . Why have you come here?

*Vilom moves towards the lamp in the niche on the left
of the front door.*

VILOM: Shall I light the lamp?

He lights the lamp with his torch.

Vilom's visit isn't such a surprising thing.

*He begins to light the lamps set along the stage front.
Ambika rises.*

AMBIKA: Go away, Vilom! You know very well that your coming here . . .

VILOM: . . . is unbearable to Mallika.

He lights more lamps and looks at Ambika.

I know, Ambika! Mallika's very innocent. She doesn't know anything about the world and about life.

He props up the torch in the bracket on the wall.

She doesn't want me to enter this house because Kalidas doesn't want me to.

He turns around and approaches Ambika.

And why doesn't Kalidas want me to come here? Because

he sees the truth of his own heart staring back at him from my eyes. He feels bewildered. . . . But you know very well, Ambika—my only flaw is that I bluntly say exactly what I feel.

AMBIKA: I don't want to discuss your faults and virtues right now.

VILOM: I can see that you're very unhappy right now. . . . And when have you not been unhappy, Ambika? Your very life is a chronicle of pain. Are you a little thinner than before? . . . I've heard that Kalidas is going to Ujjayini.

AMBIKA: I don't know.

As though he hadn't heard her, Vilom goes to the window.

VILOM: The royal court will honour Kalidas. He'll live in Ujjayini as the court poet. I think that he and Mallika should get married before he leaves. You've surely thought about this.

AMBIKA: I don't want to think about anything right now.

VILOM: You—Mallika's mother—don't wish to think about it? That's astonishing.

AMBIKA: I've told you, Vilom, you should leave.

VILOM: Kalidas will go away to Ujjayini, and Mallika—whose name has become the subject of malicious gossip all over this province because of him—will be left behind here? Right, Ambika?

Saying nothing, Ambika sits down on the window seat. Vilom turns around to face her.

Right? Have you endured all that pain for so many years only for this outcome? Even a distant observer can tell what you've had to go through all these years. Time has destroyed the unity of your mind, body, and soul. You've let yourself be consumed atom by atom, so that Mallika wouldn't experience any deprivation. And today, when deprivation for the rest of her life is the issue before you, you don't want to think at all?

AMBIKA: You aren't lessening my pain by saying all this, Vilom! I'm requesting you to leave me alone right now.

VILOM: I think it's essential for me to be with you in this situation, Ambika. I've come to say all these things—not to you, but to him. I'm hoping that he'll come here soon with Mallika. I saw Mallika going towards Jagdamba's temple. I want to wait here for her.

> *Kalidas appears in the entranceway, with Mallika behind him.*

KALIDAS: You won't have to wait very long, Vilom.

> *On seeing Vilom, Mallika's eyes fill with anger and revulsion, and she moves to the window. Kalidas draws close to Vilom.*

I know where, when, and why you eagerly look for face-to-face encounters with me. . . . Tell me, what new poetic metre are you studying these days?

VILOM: The study of poetic metres is not my inclination.

KALIDAS: Yes, I know you have a different inclination.

He looks at Vilom for a moment.

That inclination has probably separated you forever from the study of poetic metres.

VILOM: Today you can undoubtedly take pride in your study of poetic metres.

He approaches the wall and begins to fiddle with the torch in its bracket. His face glows in the torchlight.

I've heard that an invitation has come from the capital.

KALIDAS: I've heard, too. Were you unhappy?

VILOM: Unhappy? Yes, yes, very. Who isn't sorry to lose a friend? . . . Will you leave at the first auspicious opportunity tomorrow, at the crack of dawn?

KALIDAS: I don't know.

VILOM: I know perfectly well. The Acharya certainly wants to leave at the auspicious moment of dawn tomorrow. Living in luxury in the capital, you won't forget this provincial village, will you?

He glances at Mallika, then looks again at Kalidas.

I've heard that once a person reaches the city, he becomes a very busy man. Life there has so many kinds of attractions—entertainment halls, wine houses, all sorts of pleasure chambers!

Mallika's expression hardens visibly.

MALLIKA: Arya Vilom, this isn't the time or place for such talk. I didn't expect to see you here now.

VILOM: I know you aren't pleased to see me. But I came to see Ambika. We hadn't met for a long time. This isn't such an unexpected thing.

KALIDAS: Nothing that Vilom does is unexpected. What would be unexpected is his not doing a great many things.

VILOM: It's really a matter of great joy, Kalidas, that we understand each other so well. There's certainly nothing in my nature that's hidden from you.

He gazes at Kalidas for a moment.

What's Vilom? An unsuccessful Kalidas. And Kalidas? A successful Vilom. In some ways, we come very close to each other.

He moves away from the torch and approaches Kalidas.

KALIDAS: Undoubtedly. All opposites come very close to each other.

VILOM: It's good that you accept this truth. Because of the prerogative that intimacy grants me, can I ask you a question? . . . It's possible that I may never have another opportunity to talk to you. Just a day's interval will take you very far from us, won't it?

KALIDAS: Even the interval of years doesn't separate opposites from each other. . . . I'm eager to hear your question.

Vilom draws very close and places his hand on Kalidas's shoulder.

VILOM: I want to know that you're still the same Kalidas—aren't you?

He gives Ambika a meaningful look.

KALIDAS: I don't understand what you're trying to say.

He removes Vilom's hand from his shoulder.

VILOM: What I mean is—you're still the same person that you were until yesterday, aren't you?

Mallika leaves the window and advances towards them.

MALLIKA: Arya Vilom, I don't find this kind of presumption forgivable.

VILOM: Presumption?

Vilom draws close to Ambika. Kalidas moves a couple of paces in the other direction.

What's presumptuous about this? I'm asking a very meaningful question. Well, Kalidas? Isn't my question meaningful? . . . What do you think, Ambika?

Ambika gets up in an agitated state.

AMBIKA: I don't know anything about this—nor do I want to know.

She begins walking towards the inner room.

VILOM: Stop, Ambika!

Ambika stops and looks at him.

A whole lot has been said all this while, all over this village region, about Kalidas's relationship with Mallika.

Mallika takes another step forward.

MALLIKA: Arya Vilom, you . . . !

VILOM: In view of that, wouldn't it be appropriate for Kalidas to say clearly whether he's going to Ujjayini alone, or . . .

MALLIKA: Kalidas has no obligation to answer any question you ask.

VILOM: When did I say that he's obliged to answer me? But it's possible that Kalidas's conscience will compel him. Well, Kalidas?

Kalidas turns around. The two come face-to-face with each other.

KALIDAS: I certainly feel obliged to praise you. You enter not only people's homes, but also their lives, without any right to do so.

VILOM: Enter without any right? . . . I? Well, Ambika, to what extent do you agree with Kalidas's claim that I, Vilom, intrude upon people's lives without any right to do so?

AMBIKA: I've already said that I don't have anything to say about all this.

She goes into the inner room.

VILOM: That's it—she's walking away? All right, Kalidas, you tell me—to what extent do you find your own claim appropriate? Whose life have I invaded? Come, let's go to the village and ask anybody. . . .

He gives Kalidas a malevolent look. Then he goes to the torch, pulls it out of the bracket, and holds it in his hand.

So, you aren't compelled even by your conscience to answer
my question! Perhaps the question itself is such . . .

KALIDAS: You're free to speculate as you wish. All I know is that
I don't have the slightest desire to leave this rural province
and go to Ujjayini.

Vilom brings the torch close to Kalidas's face.

VILOM: Undoubtedly! Why would you have such a desire? An
ordinary person may have it, but why would you have
it? But I only want to know that, if it so happens—let's
assume for a moment that you decide to go—then, in such
a situation, isn't it appropriate that . . .

Mallika positions herself between Vilom and Kalidas.
The torchlight falls on her face.

MALLIKA: Arya Vilom, you're crossing the limit with the way
you're talking today. I'm not a child—I understand what's
in my best interest. . . . Maybe you're not aware that your
presence here right now is like that of an unwelcome guest.

VILOM: I didn't think it was necessary to be aware of that. I
know that you despise me. But I don't despise you. That's
reason enough for me to be here.

He throws the torchlight again on Kalidas's face.

There was one other thing, too, that I wanted to say to
Kalidas.

Looking meaningfully at Kalidas, he turns again to
Mallika.

You're very close to Kalidas, but I know Kalidas much
better than you.

He looks again at both of them, one by one, and moves towards the entranceway. From there, he turns around and looks once more at Kalidas.

May your journey be auspicious, Kalidas! You know that Vilom's just your well-wisher.

KALIDAS: Who can know that better than me?

A contemptuous sound escapes from Vilom's lips, and he looks at Mallika.

VILOM: It's possible that this unwanted guest may intrude again sometime. Asking your forgiveness in advance for that, too . . .

He smiles sardonically and leaves. Kalidas looks at Mallika for a moment. Then he goes to the window.

MALLIKA: You're sad again?

Kalidas continues to look out of the window.

Look, you've given me your word.

Kalidas turns back and draws close to her.

KALIDAS: Think again, Mallika. The question isn't merely one of accepting an honour and court patronage. There's a much larger question before me.

MALLIKA: And I'm that question . . . am I not?

She takes him by the arms and draws him to the window seat.

Sit down here. You know me. Don't you?

Kalidas continues to gaze at her.

Do you think I'd be happy if you spurned this opportunity, and continued to live here?

Trying to suppress her tears, she blinks and turns her gaze upwards.

I know that your departure will fill my being with emptiness. The outside world will perhaps feel very desolate, too. In spite of that, I'm not deceiving myself.

She tries to smile.

I'm saying from my heart that you should go.

KALIDAS: I wish you could see your eyes right now.

MALLIKA: My eyes are tearful because you don't understand what I'm saying.

She sits down on the floor near him and places her elbows on his knees.

Do you think you can be very far from me, even if you leave? If you stay on in this rural province, how will your talent have the opportunity to develop? The people here don't understand you. They want to test you by the standard of mediocrity.

She rests her chin on her forearm.

You believe, don't you, that I know you? I know that if any limit encircles you, you'll become confined. I don't want to confine you. That's why I say—go.

KALIDAS: You're not grasping this fully, Mallika. The question isn't one of your confining me.

*Stung by these words, Mallika still tries to retain her
composure. Kalidas gets up as though lost in thought,
and begins pacing.*

I feel that this village region is my true ground. I'm
connected to this land by many links. Among these links
are—you, this sky and these clouds, the greenery here, the
young deer, the herdsmen.

He pauses and looks at Mallika.

If I leave this place, I'll be uprooted from my land.

Mallika rests her elbows on the seat and leans on it.

MALLIKA: Why don't you consider the possibility that you'll
find the new soil richer and more fertile than the soil here?
You've already absorbed whatever you could from this
landscape. At this stage, you need new soil that will make
your self more complete.

KALIDAS: A new land could also dry me up.

He begins pacing again.

MALLIKA: There's no soil that doesn't contain a measure of
freshness. Your imagination will certainly find a way to be
touched by that freshness.

KALIDAS: And that life will also come with its own
expectations. . . .

*Rising and drawing close to him, Mallika takes his
hands in her own.*

MALLIKA: Why is it necessary for you to fulfil those expectations?
You can create your own new expectations in others.

KALIDAS: Even so, a lot of doubts and apprehensions keep cropping up. I don't feel any enthusiasm in my heart.

MALLIKA: Look at me.

Kalidas gazes into her eyes for several moments.

You still don't feel any enthusiasm . . . ? Believe me, you won't be separated from this place even after you've gone away. The wind, the clouds, the deer of this landscape— you'll take them all with you. . . . And I, too, won't be far from you—I'll be gathered up in the clouds that come floating by.

Lightning flashes and the sound of thunder can be heard. Kalidas continues to hold her hands. Mallika tries to control her tears by blinking.

It looks like rain, again. As it is, it has grown very dark. The Acharya must be waiting for you.

KALIDAS: Are you asking me to leave?

MALLIKA: Yes! You'll see—after you've left, I'll be cheerful, I'll wander about a lot, and every evening I'll go to Jagdamba's temple, to watch the sunset. . . .

KALIDAS: This means that I should take my leave of you.

MALLIKA: No! I'm not going to give you leave. Because you're going, I'll only pray that your passage may be praiseworthy.

She lets go of his hands.

Go.

Kalidas keeps his eyes closed for a few moments. Then

he turns abruptly and leaves. Hiding her face in her hands, Mallika goes to the window seat and sits down. Loud thunder is heard in the background and, with that, the sounds of rain beginning. Mallika tries to control herself, but begins to sob. Ambika emerges from the interior and puts her hand on Mallika's head. Then she raises Mallika's face.

AMBIKA: Mallika!

Mallika rises from the seat and, moving to the window, leans her head against its frame.

You're not well, Mallika. Come inside and rest.

Mallika remains standing in that posture, trying to control her sobs.

MALLIKA: Let me stay here, Ma. I'm not unwell. Look, Ma, what dense clouds have gathered all around us! Tomorrow, these clouds will travel towards Ujjayini. . . .

She sobs again with her face in her hands. Ambika goes to her and holds her close.

AMBIKA: Don't weep, Mallika.

MALLIKA: I'm not weeping, Ma. What's pouring from my eyes isn't grief. It's happiness, Ma, happiness. . . .

She hides her face on Ambika's breast. The sound of thunder again, and the noise of rain growing louder.

End of Act One

Act Two

Some years later.

The same room. The condition of the room has changed perceptibly. The plaster is peeling in several places. The swastikas, conch shells, and lotuses painted in vermilion are now faded. There are far fewer pots and pans around the stove. There are only two clay jars, and they are now covered completely with moss. A few pages of bark manuscript are scattered on the seat near the window, and some more pages are wrapped in silk. There is a broken round cane stool near the seat, on which lies a blank book made of bark sheets sewn together. In a corner near the stove is a clothes line, on which a few clothes are spread out to dry. Most of the clothes are torn, and covered all over with patches.

Another broken round cane stool is placed near the entranceway. There is only one square stool left, on which Mallika sits, grinding medicinal herbs in a stone mortar. The corner of the bed in the inner room is visible as before. Ambika is lying on the bed. Every now and then, she turns on her side. Nikshep enters. Mallika adjusts her wrap.

NIKSHEP: How's Ambika's health now?

MALLIKA: She still runs a fever, as before.

NIKSHEP: There's no difference, compared to earlier?

MALLIKA: Doesn't look like it.

NIKSHEP: The same recurring illness, for two years running!

> *Mallika sighs with resignation, and begins to pour the powdered medicine from the mortar into a bowl. Nikshep drags the second cane stool and sits down near her.*

Ambika really worries too much.

MALLIKA: She also doesn't take her medicine properly.

> *She adds milk and honey to the medicine and stirs it. Nikshep sits with his fingers intertwined, gazing at her.*

NIKSHEP: How's your health?

MALLIKA: It's okay.

NIKSHEP: You're getting thinner. . . . No one has come from the capital for a long time.

> *Mallika averts her eyes and keeps stirring the medicine busily.*

I sometimes think that I should go to Ujjayini and meet him.

MALLIKA: Why?

NIKSHEP: I want to talk to him about a lot of things. I often feel that it's all my fault.

Mallika looks at him gravely.

MALLIKA: What's your fault?

Nikshep sighs deeply.

NIKSHEP: You know what it is. . . . I didn't expect Kalidas to go to Ujjayini and just lose himself there like this.

MALLIKA: And I'm very happy that he's so busy with his life there. Here he wrote only *A Gathering of Seasons*. There he has composed several new long poems. The merchants who came this way two years ago brought me copies of *The Origin of the Young God* and *The Cloud-Messenger*. They said there was a lot of talk about another long poem of his, but they couldn't get a copy of it.

NIKSHEP: For that matter, I've heard that he has also written some plays that have been performed in Ujjayini's entertainment halls. Even so . . .

MALLIKA: Even so, what?

NIKSHEP: It pains me to say this. We also heard so many other things from the lips of the same travelling merchants . . .

MALLIKA: When a man prospers, gossip of all sorts gets attached to his name.

NIKSHEP: I'm not talking about mere gossip.

He gets up and starts pacing.

We also heard, didn't we, that he was married to a princess of the Gupta dynasty.

MALLIKA: So, what's wrong with that?

NIKSHEP: From one angle, there's nothing wrong. But what about his insistence while he was here—that he'd never get married?

He pauses and looks at Mallika.

What happened to that assertion? Didn't he realize that it was to honour his vow that you . . . ?

MALLIKA: In relation to him, I don't figure anywhere. I'm one among countless ordinary people. He's extraordinary. He needed someone extraordinary as his companion in life. . . . I hear that the princess is very learned.

NIKSHEP: Yes, I've heard. She has studied many philosophies and disciplines. I said, didn't I, that from one angle, there's nothing wrong with this situation. But, looking at it from another angle, one feels a great deal of remorse.

MALLIKA: On the contrary, I feel an aversion to myself—because, being what I am, I could have become an obstacle to his success. If I hadn't encouraged him to leave at your urging, what a great loss it would have been!

NIKSHEP: That's exactly why I'm sad—if you hadn't done this at my urging, your life wouldn't have acquired this shape today.

MALLIKA: How's my life different from what it was? Earlier, Ma used to do the work. Now she's unwell, and I do the work.

NIKSHEP: That's all the difference one can see on the outside.

MALLIKA: That's all the difference.

She stands up with the medicine.

Let me give Ma her medicine. I'll be right back.

*She goes in and, helping Ambika to sit up, feeds her
the medicine. Ambika swallows, then shakes her head.
Nikshep strolls over to the lattice window. Outside,
the sound of horses' hooves approaches, then recedes.
Nikshep continues to watch from the window. Having
taken her medicine, Ambika lies down. Mallika
emerges from the inner room, and turns in the doorway
to look at Ambika.*

MALLIKA: Ma, if you're cold, shall I shut the door?

*Ambika nods. Mallika shuts the door. Nikshep steps
away from the window.*

NIKSHEP: Looks like some outsiders are visiting us again today.

MALLIKA: Who?

NIKSHEP: They're probably royal court officials. I noticed a
couple of figures like the ones we'd seen when the Acharya
came to fetch Kalidas.

A shiver runs through Mallika.

MALLIKA: The same kind of figures?

Suppressing her mood, she tries to laugh.

Do you know what Ma says about this? She says that
whenever these figures appear, some calamity or other
strikes us. Sometimes a war, sometimes an epidemic! . . .
But nothing of the sort happened last time.

NIKSHEP: Didn't happen?

*Averting her eyes again, Mallika busies herself with
checking the damp clothes on the line.*

MALLIKA: What happened? . . . And whatever happened was
for the best.

*She removes one or two garments from the clothes line,
then spreads them out on the line again.*

It's so humid these days that clothes don't dry for hours.

*The sound of hooves is heard once more. Nikshep
goes to the window once more. Suddenly, he exclaims
in surprise.*

NIKSHEP: What . . . what? . . . No? . . . But how not?

*The sound of hooves recedes into the distance. Nikshep
steps away from the window in agitation.*

MALLIKA: Why are you suddenly agitated, Arya Nikshep?

NIKSHEP: I've just seen another figure passing by on horseback.

MALLIKA: So what? Like Ma, are you also dreading a disaster?

NIKSHEP: That's a very familiar figure, Mallika!

MALLIKA: A familiar figure?

NIKSHEP: I'm sure it's Kalidas himself.

Mallika freezes, still clutching the clothes in her hand.

MALLIKA: Kalidas? . . . How's that possible?

NIKSHEP: I saw him with my own eyes. He has gone galloping
towards the mountain peak. Others may not be able to
recognize him in his royal garb, but Nikshep's eyes can't be

mistaken. . . . I'll go and look right away. The court officials must have come with him.

Nikshep leaves in the same state of agitation.

MALLIKA: He's here, and he has gone towards the mountain peak?

She bites her finger, and, experiencing pain, walks mechanically towards the window, as though in a daze. Rangini and Sangini appear in the entranceway. Mallika looks at them in surprise. Rangini pushes Sangini forward.

RANGINI: Ask her, can we come in?

Sangini pushes Rangini forward, and steps back herself.

SANGINI: You ask.

Mallika approaches them.

RANGINI: Okay, I'll ask. . . . Look here, is this your home?

MALLIKA: Yes, yes. Please come in. . . . Have you come to visit me?

Rangini and Sangini enter the room, and look around with searching eyes.

RANGINI: We haven't come to visit anyone in particular. Just think of it this way—we're here for no reason at all, we're just wandering about the countryside.

SANGINI: We want to see the homes around here.

RANGINI: And we want to study the life here.

SANGINI: Let me perform the introductions first. This is Rangini. She's a student of dance at the theatre academy in Ujjayini. She's also interested in writing plays.

RANGINI: And this is Sangini—she's learning how to play the *mridanga* and the *veena* at the same academy. She writes very beautiful love songs. Now she's inclining towards prose. And how do you introduce yourself?

Mallika does not answer, and continues to stare at them in astonishment.

SANGINI: You haven't introduced yourself.

MALLIKA: I have nothing to introduce. Please come, take this seat here.

SANGINI: We've come here to study, not to sit down. What do you people call this kind of space?

MALLIKA: Which space?

RANGINI: She means this entire space where we are at this moment. In Ujjayini we call this a room. What do you people call it here?

MALLIKA: A room.

RANGINI: You people also call a room a room? And . . .

Going up to the large clay jars, she touches one of them.

. . . this?

MALLIKA: A jar.

RANGINI: A jar. You call a room a room, and a jar a jar?

She shrugs her shoulders in disappointment.

SANGINI: Look, don't you have any local words here?

Mallika continues to stare at them in bewilderment.

MALLIKA: Local words?

SANGINI: Yes. Regional dialect words. Don't you know—the great Sanskrit grammarian, Patanjali, has noted that some people say *yenn* for *when*, and *zenn* for *then*. As he states, '*Yenn* is *yenn* and *zenn* is *zenn*.'

MALLIKA: I don't possess such great learning.

Sangini sits down on the window seat with a somewhat disappointed look. Rangini walks around the room, inspecting each and every object closely. Mallika goes up to Sangini.

SANGINI: Look, we want to learn a few things that are connected to life in this place, and this place only. Your homes and clothing are almost like ours. What's truly special about life here?

MALLIKA: Truly special about life here?

For a moment she looks towards the window.

I don't know. From every angle, our life's very ordinary.

SANGINI: I can't accept that. This region has given birth to an extraordinary talent like Kalidas. Each and every thing here ought to be extraordinary.

After examining all the objects around the stove carefully, and after peeking into the inner room, Rangini rejoins Sangini.

RANGINI: Look, let me explain to you. The thing is that, by royal order, we're both doing research on the background of poet Kalidas's life. You can understand what a big and important task this is. But, after wandering about this place, we're almost in despair, because there's no material here at all.

SANGINI: Okay, tell us the names of some of the local plants.

MALLIKA: What kinds of plants?

RANGINI: What kinds of plants?

She begins to ponder.

As Kalidas has written in his poem *The Origin of the Young God*, 'great healing herbs are radiant jewels'. What are these medicinal herbs that emit light?

MALLIKA: Medicinal herbs don't emit light.

Sangini rises abruptly.

SANGINI: Medicinal herbs don't emit light? Do you mean to say that what Kalidas has written is false?

MALLIKA: He hasn't written anything that's false. What he has actually written is that . . .

RANGINI: Let it be, Sangini! She doesn't really know much about this place.

Sangini also rises, with a grimace of disappointment.

SANGINI: Okay, we've wasted a lot of your time. Forgive us. Let's go, Rangini!

Both leave. Mallika shuts the front door. She sits down on the floor near the window seat, and rests her head

*on the scattered pages of bark manuscript. She closes
her eyes.*

MALLIKA: You've come back today after so many years. I used
to think that, on the day of your return, the clouds would
be gathered in the same way, the day would be dark in the
same way, I'd get drenched in the rain again in the same
way, and I'd say to you—look, I've read all your poems . . .

She picks up a few pages.

How often have I begged the merchants travelling to
Ujjayini to bring back copies of your poems for me! . . . I
used to think that I'd sing verses from *The Cloud-Messenger*
to you. That the temple bells would ring out from the
mountain peak, and I'd place this gift from me in your
hands . . .

She picks up the blank book lying on the round stool.

That I'd say—look, this is for your next work. I've prepared
these blank bark pages and stitched them together with my
own hands. Whenever and whatever you write on them,
I'll feel that I, too, am present somewhere, that I, too, have
something.

She heaves a sigh, and puts down the book.

But now that you're here today, the whole atmosphere's
quite different. And . . . and I'm unable to understand if
you yourself are the same, or . . . ?

*Someone knocks on the door. She gets up quickly,
straightening her clothes, and opens the door.*

*Anusvar and Anunasik appear in the entranceway,
standing together. Mallika looks at them with
incomprehension.*

ANUSVAR: I'm certain I'm standing before the lady Mallika at
this moment.

MALLIKA: Yes—go ahead.

ANUSVAR: Please accept greetings from the servants of Lord
Matrugupta.

*They both greet her with a deep bow. Mallika continues
to gape at them.*

MALLIKA: Lord Matrugupta? Who's this Lord Matrugupta?

ANUSVAR: The lord of poets, the creator of *A Gathering of
Seasons*, *The Origin of the Young God*, *The Cloud-Messenger*,
and *Raghu's Dynasty*, the scholar who's a master of politics
and the future governor of Kashmir. Lord Matrugupta's
royal consort, a daughter of the Gupta dynasty, the
supremely accomplished lady Priyangumanjari, is eager
to be in your august presence, and desires to arrive here
shortly. We, her minions, are here to give you advance
notice of her arrival.

MALLIKA: The author of *A Gathering of Seasons*, *The Cloud-
Messenger*, and so forth, is Kalidas, but you're saying that . . .

ANUSVAR: He's on his way to take up the governorship of
Kashmir, on behalf of the Gupta dynasty. His new name's
Matrugupta.

MALLIKA: He's going to be the governor of Kashmir? And . . . and . . . his royal consort's coming to meet me?

ANUSVAR: I'm sure that, on this proud occasion, you'll consider it essential to carry out a few changes in the arrangement of objects in the room where you receive your guests. Taking this as your command, we'll accomplish the task with our own hands right away. Come, Anunasik.

Entering the room, the two of them begin to examine all the objects with an eye to managing the change. Mallika moves aside, to be out of their way. Anunasik goes up to the window seat.

ANUNASIK: In my opinion, this seat should be near the front door.

ANUSVAR: The princess will enter through the door, and the seat will be right next to it?

ANUNASIK: In that case, this seat should be moved from its present position seven finger-widths to the south.

ANUSVAR: To the south?

He shakes his head in disagreement.

In my opinion, its position should be five finger-widths to the north. The sun's rays fall directly upon it through the window.

ANUNASIK: I don't concur with you.

ANUSVAR: I don't concur with you.

ANUNASIK: So?

ANUSVAR: So, because the issue is contentious, the seat should be left where it is.

ANUNASIK: Okay, then. Let it remain where it is. And these jars?

He goes up to the jars.

ANUSVAR: In my opinion, one jar should be in this corner, and the other in that corner.

ANUNASIK: But, in my opinion, the jars shouldn't be here at all.

ANUSVAR: Why?

ANUNASIK: There's no answer to 'why'.

ANUSVAR: I don't concur with you.

ANUNASIK: I don't concur with you.

ANUSVAR: So?

ANUNASIK: So, the jars should also be left where they are.

They both go towards the area where clothes have been spread out to dry on a line. Mallika gathers up the manuscript pages scattered near the window seat, places them on the round stool, and goes quietly into the inner room. Anusvar touches the damp clothes.

ANUSVAR: These clothes?

ANUNASIK: The clothes are still damp, so they shouldn't be removed.

ANUSVAR: Why?

ANUNASIK: That's the standard procedure, according to the canonical books.

ANUSVAR: What standard procedure is that?

ANUNASIK: That I don't remember.

ANUSVAR: But you do remember that such a standard procedure exists?

ANUNASIK: Yes.

ANUSVAR: So?

ANUNASIK: So, this is an obscure and dubious topic.

ANUSVAR: Yes, it's certainly an obscure and dubious topic.

ANUNASIK: Since the whole subject is so dubious, the clothes, too, should be left where they are.

ANUSVAR: Okay, then. The clothes, too, should be left where they are.

ANUNASIK: But this stove must definitely be moved from its present position.

ANUSVAR: Moving the stove would mean that all the objects around it would also have to be moved. That would take a lot of time.

ANUNASIK: In addition to time, it would take a lot of patience.

ANUSVAR: In addition to patience, it would take a lot of physical labour.

ANUNASIK: In my opinion, handling pots and pans is not appropriate for people of our rank and station.

ANUSVAR: I have exactly the same opinion.

ANUNASIK: So, do we both concur that the stove shouldn't be moved from its present position?

ANUSVAR: In my opinion, we both concur.

Anunasik looks all around the room.

ANUNASIK: There's nothing else left to be done, is there?

Anusvar also looks all around the room.

ANUSVAR: In my opinion, there's nothing else left to be done.

ANUNASIK: No—there's something left.

ANUSVAR: What?

ANUNASIK: This square stool's lying in the way here. It should be removed from its present position.

ANUSVAR: I concur.

ANUNASIK: So?

ANUSVAR: So?

ANUNASIK: So, it should be removed.

ANUSVAR: Yes, it should definitely be removed.

ANUNASIK: So?

ANUSVAR: So?

ANUNASIK: Remove it.

ANUSVAR: Who—me?

ANUNASIK: Yes.

ANUSVAR: Not you?

ANUNASIK: No.

ANUSVAR: Why?

ANUNASIK: There's no answer to 'why'.

ANUSVAR: Even so!

ANUNASIK: I asked you first.

ANUSVAR: But you noticed the stool first.

ANUNASIK: So?

ANUSVAR: So?

ANUNASIK: Move it.

ANUSVAR: You move it.

ANUNASIK: Then let it be.

ANUSVAR: Let it be.

ANUNASIK: What now?

ANUSVAR: Yes, what now?

ANUNASIK: Let's review everything once more.

ANUSVAR: Yes, let's review everything once more.

Matul enters in an agitated state.

MATUL: Members of the official class, has your work here been duly completed?

ANUNASIK: What say you, Anusvar?

ANUSVAR: Yes, it has been duly completed. It has, hasn't it? What say you, Anunasik?

ANUNASIK: Yes, it's all done. All that's left is to review everything once more.

ANUSVAR: Yes, all that's left is to review everything once more.

MATUL: Then let that review be, for now. Princess Priyangumanjari has arrived outside.

ANUNASIK: The princess has arrived outside! Then let's go,
Anusvar.

ANUSVAR: Let's go.

> *Both walk out together. Matul also follows them, and
> returns in a few moments, showing Priyangumanjari
> the way.*

MATUL: She's the most virtuous, most humble, and most
innocent girl in the whole region. . . .

> *Mallika emerges from the inner room.*

Come, come, Mallika! I was just singing your praises to
the princess.

> *He laughs obsequiously.*

From the moment she arrived, the princess has been asking
only about you. . . . So this is our Mallika, the royal swan
of this province. Um . . . um . . . Mallika, which seat has
been chosen for the princess?

> *Mallika ceremonially greets Priyangumanjari, who
> smiles and acknowledges the greeting.*

PRIYANGUMANJARI: Arya Matul, you should go and rest now.
The attendants will wait outside until I'm ready to return.

MATUL: But a seat for you . . . ?

PRIYANGUMANJARI: Please don't worry about that. I won't be
inconvenienced.

MATUL: Of course, you'll be inconvenienced. It's quite another thing if you choose not to consider an inconvenience an inconvenience. And this, in fact, is what's called nobility. The mark of a noble family is precisely that . . .

PRIYANGUMANJARI: Please go and rest. I've already tired you out a great deal.

MATUL: Tired me out? You have?

He laughs obsequiously again.

Would I be tired out by you? Even if you were to tell me to go up and down between the bottom of a gorge and the top of a mountain all day long, I still wouldn't get tired. Matul's body is made of iron—solid iron. I won't indulge in self-praise, but, in addition to intellectual brilliance, our clan also possesses a great deal of physical strength. I've often covered ten leagues in a day while tending to my herds. I say that the hardest work in the world is raising a herd. If even one animal strays from the path, then . . .

PRIYANGUMANJARI: Look, your animals must be wandering off today as well. Please go and check on them at least once.

MATUL: Do you think I still look after animals? A connection with the Gupta dynasty—and the tending of animals? I sold off all my animals years ago. And, truth be told, even that turned out to be profitable for me, because . . .

Priyangumanjari's gaze meets Mallika's. She advances and takes Mallika's hands in her own.

PRIYANGUMANJARI: You're really just the way I'd imagined you.

Somewhat perturbed, Mallika continues to stare at her.

MATUL: Because . . . oh . . . oh . . . okay. Then please give me leave. There are a lot of things scattered around in my house. I have to make a lot of different arrangements. So the attendants will wait for you. . . . Even so, if you have any orders for me, please send me word. . . . Mallika, do make some arrangement for the princess to sit down. Otherwise, she'll remain standing like this. Okay, I'm leaving. If you have any orders, please let me know.

PRIYANGUMANJARI: You should go. There's no need to worry about anything here.

MATUL: Okay . . . okay . . . !

He starts on the way out.

Why do I need to worry? Mallika's here to do the worrying—and Ambika too. . . . Even so, if you have any task for me, please let me know. . . .

He exits. Priyangumanjari gazes at Mallika for a moment, and then reaches out and touches her chin.

PRIYANGUMANJARI: You're really very beautiful. Do you know, even though we're not acquainted, you don't seem unfamiliar to me.

MALLIKA: Please sit down, won't you?

PRIYANGUMANJARI: No, I don't want to sit down. I want to look at you and your home. He has talked about you and this house numerous times. He'd recall this place very often while composing *The Cloud-Messenger*.

*Her gaze circles around the room, and settles again
on Mallika's face.*

Today, it's precisely the attraction of this land that has
brought us here. Otherwise, it would have been more
convenient for us to travel by a different route.

MALLIKA: I can't figure out what I should do to welcome you
as a guest. If you'll take a seat, I'll . . .

PRIYANGUMANJARI: Don't worry about hospitality. I haven't come
to your home as a guest. . . . It was quite possible that he
wouldn't have come here, but I've brought him back with
a lot of special pleading. I wanted to see this region for
myself at least once. Besides . . .

A sound of suppressed anguish escapes her lips.

. . . besides, there was another reason. I wanted to carry
away some of the atmosphere of this place with me.

MALLIKA: The atmosphere of this place?

*Priyangumanjari looks at her with a smile, and then
strolls to the window.*

PRIYANGUMANJARI: One can see even very distant mountain
ranges from here. . . . What unsullied beauty! Ever since I
arrived here, I've been feeling envious of you.

Mallika advances a couple of steps towards her.

MALLIKA: It would be our good fortune if you'd stay in this
region for a few days. Of course, you'll face inconveniences
here, but . . .

Priyangumanjari looks at her again with a pained expression.

PRIYANGUMANJARI: All of life's conveniences seem trivial before this beauty. Even a whole lifetime isn't enough to drink it in with one's eyes.

She moves away from the window.

But where are the time and leisure to do so? The politics of Kashmir is so unstable that our staying away from it for a single day can create a host of problems. . . . The governorship of an entire province is an enormous responsibility. Our responsibility's even greater, because the situation in Kashmir is extremely dangerous at the moment. In a way, there's just as much talk about the beauty of Kashmir, but where will we have the leisure to view it?

She sits down on the window seat, and leans back on her arms.

That's why I'm envious of you. This easy enjoyment of beauty is a mere dream for us. . . . Sit down.

She gestures to Mallika to sit beside her on the window seat. When Mallika moves to sit on the floor, Priyangumanjari stops her.

Sit here—next to me.

MALLIKA: Let me get another seat.

She picks up a stool from the corner, places it next to the window seat, and sits down, gathering into her lap the bark manuscript pages that were lying on it.

PRIYANGUMANJARI: It seems that, even though you live in this rural province, you have an attachment to literature.

Mallika lowers her eyes.

Whose works are these?

MALLIKA: Kalidas's.

Priyangumanjari's eyebrows contract slightly.

PRIYANGUMANJARI: Now he's known as Matrugupta. Are his works available even here?

MALLIKA: I've obtained these copies from merchants travelling from Ujjayini.

A slightly sarcastic smile appears on Priyangumanjari's lips.

PRIYANGUMANJARI: I can understand that. I've learnt from him that you've been his companion since childhood. Your attraction towards his works is natural.

She begins to look at the ceiling, as though lost in thought.

Whenever he talks about this place, he becomes totally self-absorbed. That's why his mind often begins to lose interest in political matters.

Her eyes settle on Mallika's face again.

On such occasions, one has to make a great effort to keep his mind on an even keel. Politics isn't literature. In politics, each and every moment is vital. If ever there's even a momentary lapse, it can result in great harm. To keep his groove in political life, a person needs to be extremely vigilant. . . . Literature was the first phase of his life. Now he has entered the second phase. Most of my time's spent in an effort to ensure that this step forward doesn't become a step back. . . . This involves a lot of hard work.

She tries to smile.

Don't you think that's right?

MALLIKA: I don't know anything about life in politics.

PRIYANGUMANJARI: Because you've always lived in a rural region.

She stands up abruptly. When Mallika also begins to get up, Priyangumanjari stops her by placing a hand on her shoulder, and makes her sit down again.

Keep sitting.

She walks around, biting her lower lip.

I told you I want to carry away some of the atmosphere of this place with me. That's because I don't want him to feel he's missing something. Such a feeling often causes a lot of damage. He unnecessarily loses his composure, which wastes both time and energy. His time's very valuable. I don't want his time to be wasted in that way.

She pauses before Mallika.

That's why I'm taking a lot of things from here with me. We'll take some fawns, which we'll rear in our garden. The medicinal herbs from here will be planted in the garden pavilion and the surrounding areas. We'll also have some houses in the style of this region constructed there. Matul and his family, too, will accompany us. We'll take some orphans from here and educate them there. I think all this will make a difference.

She strolls over to the other side of the room.

I see that your home's in a pretty dilapidated state. Its restoration is essential. If you want, I'll issue orders for this task before I leave. Two skilled builders have come with us from Ujjayini. What do you say?

Mallika rises and approaches her.

MALLIKA: You're very generous. But we're used to living in a home like this, so we don't find it inconvenient.

PRIYANGUMANJARI: Even so, I'd like to have this house restored. The early years of his life had a connection with this home as well. I've already ordered the construction of a new mansion in place of Matul's house. I've told the builders to get stone of the finest quality from Ujjayini and start the work. Regrettably, I won't be able to stay back and supervise the work in person. We'll have to begin the rest of our journey tomorrow. . . . Why don't you come along with us?

Mallika stares at her incomprehendingly.

MALLIKA: Me?

Priyangumanjari draws near and places a hand on her shoulder.

PRIYANGUMANJARI: Yes! What's standing in the way? You're not really bound to this place with any such thread that . . .

MALLIKA: My mother's here.

PRIYANGUMANJARI: That's no obstacle. Arrangements can be made to take your mother along as well. Our builders will work on the renovation of this house, and you'll live there with me as my companion.

An expression of hurt pride appears on Mallika's face.
But she continues to keep herself in check.

MALLIKA: I beg your pardon. I don't consider myself worthy of such an honour.

PRIYANGUMANJARI: But I believe you're worthy of much more than this. . . . Before I arrived, two court officials had come here.

A twisted smile appears again on her lips.

I didn't send them as a mere formality. Have you seen both of them?

Trying to figure out her meaning, Mallika looks at her uncertainly.

MALLIKA: I've seen them.

PRIYANGUMANJARI: We can arrange for your marriage to whichever one of them you find suitable. They are both capable officials.

MALLIKA: Your Highness!

Clutching the bark manuscript pages to her chest, she retreats a few steps towards the window seat. Giving her a level look, Priyangumanjari walks slowly towards her.

PRIYANGUMANJARI: It's possible that you find neither of them suitable. But these aren't the only two officials in the kingdom—there are many others. Come with me. Anyone you wish to marry . . .

> *Mallika sits down on the window seat and, with suppressed agitation, bites her lip.*

MALLIKA: Please stop discussing this subject.

> *Because her voice has become hoarse, the words are not clearly audible. The door to the inner room opens and Ambika appears, weak and trembling with illness and rage; then she stops, as though to gather herself.*

PRIYANGUMANJARI: Why? Don't you have a vision of a home and a family of your own?

> *Ambika advances slowly towards them.*

AMBIKA: No. She has no such vision.

> *Priyangumanjari turns around to look at Ambika. Mallika rises in a state of agitation.*

MALLIKA: Ma!

AMBIKA: She has no such vision in her head because she lives at the level of pure emotion. For her, in life . . .

> *She becomes breathless, and the words catch in her throat. Mallika puts down the manuscript pages on the window seat and, going up to Ambika, supports her by the back.*

MALLIKA: Why did you get up and come out, Ma? You're not keeping well. Come, lie down inside.

Mallika wants to take Ambika back into the inner room, but Ambika pushes Mallika's arm off her back.

AMBIKA: Can't I even talk to a visitor? I've been suffocating here for days, months, years. For me this home isn't a home, but a cave of death in which I'm locked up all the time. And you don't even want me to talk to anybody?

In an effort to walk, she stumbles. Mallika holds her up.

MALLIKA: But, Ma, you're not well.

AMBIKA: I'm in better health than you are.

She walks up to Priyangumanjari and looks her up and down.

This home hasn't always been in this condition, princess! When I was still active, I used to keep it spick and span every day. Everything here hadn't gone to wrack and ruin like this. But, nowadays, even the two of us, mother and daughter, just lie here, as though we've gone to pieces. All this, because . . .

Out of breath again, she's unable to speak further. Priyangumanjari moves away from her on the pretext of looking around the room.

PRIYANGUMANJARI: I can see that this house isn't in good condition. If Mallika could come with me, the problem would be solved easily. But now . . .

Biting her lip, she pauses for a moment, as though to think.

I'll still do whatever's possible before I leave. I'll instruct the builders to demolish this house, and in its place . . .

Mallika recoils.

MALLIKA: Please don't do that. Please don't give the order to demolish this house.

Priyangumanjari gives her a level look again.

PRIYANGUMANJARI: I was saying that only out of consideration for you. If it's inconvenient, then . . . it's all right. I won't issue such an order. Still, I want to do something or the other for you. I can't stay any longer now. I have to finish several essential tasks before tomorrow's journey. I didn't really have the time even now. But I felt it was necessary to visit you. He had gone for a ride towards the mountain peak, and while he was away, I came here. All right, then . . . !

Mallika wrings her hands and lowers her eyes. In her anger, Ambika takes a couple of steps towards Priyangumanjari.

AMBIKA: I wanted to say something to you, princess. I wanted to tell you that we people . . . we people . . .

She begins coughing, and her words are drowned out by the cough. Priyangumanjari turns at the front door to look at her.

PRIYANGUMANJARI: I understand your pain. I'll certainly help you in any way I can. Right now, the attendants are waiting for me, so . . .

She looks at Mallika with a sombre smile, shakes her head, and leaves. Limp with emotion, Ambika

*continues to look in Priyangumanjari's direction.
Then she practically collapses on to the window seat,
picks up some manuscript pages, and holds them out
to Mallika.*

AMBIKA: Here, read the lines from *The Cloud-Messenger*. Didn't
you say that the tenderness of his inner self was embodied
in them? Haven't you seen an even more embodied form
of that tenderness today?

Mallika stares at her, as though transfixed.

When he wants to pay you the true worth of your pure
emotion today, why don't you accept it? The four walls of
this house will be restored, and you'll be able to live in their
household as a servant. What better fortune do you want?

MALLIKA: The princess has her own outlook on life, Ma. How
can someone else be held responsible for it?

AMBIKA: But who's responsible for the princess's visit here? She
undoubtedly came here in accordance with that person's
wishes. The court's builders will renovate this house! Today
he's in power, he has wealth. What better means could he
have for acquainting us with that power and wealth?

MALLIKA: But, Ma . . .

AMBIKA: Ma knows nothing, understands nothing. Ma can't
plumb the depths of feeling, Ma . . .

*She starts coughing again, and can't speak further.
Vilom comes in from outside.*

VILOM: Why are you so upset, Ambika . . . ? The whole village
is envying you your good fortune today.

He gives Mallika a meaningful look. She avoids his gaze and moves to the other side.

When the dust of royal feet blesses a house, people feel a great deal of pride. An occasion like this doesn't turn up in everybody's life, does it?

AMBIKA: I've lived my life up to this day only to witness this occasion! How can such great good fortune fit into our mean little life?

She gets up abruptly.

Come, I'll go to the village and broadcast our good fortune in person to everybody. So many years of deprivation and pain have brought forth such big fruit that royal builders are going to renovate our house!

VILOM: Sit down, Ambika! The village has no time to listen to you today.

He strolls over to the window.

The people of the village are busy at this time. They've got to put together a lot of different things for the guests who've come from elsewhere. Today, those guests want to collect and cart away even the stones of this place. The stones of this place are now considered extremely valuable.

MALLIKA: The stones of this place were valuable earlier, too, Arya Vilom. It's a different matter that no one grasped their value before now.

Ambika angrily takes several steps towards Mallika.

AMBIKA: So why don't you go and collect some for yourself?

It's possible that people may not leave a single stone in this place, and then there will be nothing left to support your emotion.

MALLIKA: Sit down, Ma, your condition isn't good.

> *Holding Ambika by the arm, Mallika steers her to the window seat.*

VILOM: There's a lot of excitement all over the village. This is the most festive day in the life of the region. People aren't worrying about their animals today. They're busy putting together food and drink for the visitors. Among these materials are also some fawns that are being rounded up on the special orders of the princess.

MALLIKA: That's not true.

VILOM: Not true? The princess herself has ordered Indravarma and Vishnudutt to . . .

MALLIKA: That order could have some other meaning, too.

VILOM: Some other meaning? What other meaning can it have? Will the princess play with those fawns or will the artists of Ujjayini paint their likenesses? It's an entertaining spectacle that the artists from the capital city accompanying the royal family are wandering about today, creating copies of every object in our village. They won't leave a single tree, leaf or blade of grass here—of which they haven't created and carried away a copy.

MALLIKA: This, too, could have some other meaning.

> *Vilom leaves the window and draws closer to Mallika.*

VILOM: When did I say that there's no other meaning? The meaning's very clear. They see every object here as a representation of strangeness, and they want to take that strangeness from here and display it to others. You, me, this house, these mountains—for them, these are all examples of the strange and the exotic. I, for one, commend their subtle and skilful vision, which can see strangeness even where no strangeness exists. I saw an artist today painting a portrait of his own shadow in the sunlight of this place.

AMBIKA: In the sunlight here they must find their own shadows unfamiliar! . . . Who was that demoness who used to catch hold of every creature by its shadow?

> *She starts wheezing again as she talks.*

I wish I were that demoness, so that today I could . . . today I could . . .

> *Her coughing drowns her words. Mallika goes to her and supports her by the shoulders.*

MALLIKA: I've told you, Ma, you should rest. Don't talk. . . . Arya Vilom, Ma isn't feeling well. Please let her rest now.

VILOM: Yes, take Ambika inside. The noise of the festivities in the village will disturb her mind even more. I came only to inform you about the celebrations. I'm surprised that Kalidas didn't consider it appropriate to visit you. I've heard that those people will actually leave tomorrow.

AMBIKA: He didn't think it appropriate to visit us because he knows that Ambika's still alive.

VILOM: But I believe he'll certainly come here once. He ought to come. No one breaks a bond in this manner.

He strolls over to the window again.

And, especially, no one who possesses a poet's tender heart. What do you think, Mallika? Shouldn't he come here once?

MALLIKA: Arya Vilom, I've requested you to let Ma rest right now. Your talk unsettles Ma's mind.

VILOM: My talk unsettles Ambika's mind? I believe that the sources of the disturbance lie elsewhere. Ambika knows the reasons why her mind is unsettled.

He looks out of the window.

I also understand those causes. That's why I come out and say many of the things that remain buried in Ambika's mind.

He turns to look at Mallika.

I know you find my presence disagreeable. That's nothing new. But I want to stay just a little longer.

He looks out again.

I see a horseman coming down from the mountain peak. It's possible that, this time, he'll want to stop here for a few moments. In that event, I'll also ask after his welfare. He and I have an old friendship.

Mallika begins to lose control of herself.

MALLIKA: Arya Vilom, in that case your presence here wouldn't be appropriate at all, from any perspective. If you'd like to meet him, this isn't the only place to do so.

Vilom continues to look out of the window as before.

VILOM: But what's wrong with this place? This is exactly where we met the day he left. The passage of time will be imperceptible if we meet in the same spot after so many years.

Mallika goes up to Vilom, and, taking him by the arm, wants to draw him away from the window.

MALLIKA: I request you not to be obstinate right now about staying here. . . .

Vilom does not budge from his position. The sound of hooves becomes audible in the distance.

I'm asking you to please go away. This is my house. I don't want you to be in my house right now.

Vilom remains standing as before. The sound of hooves keeps drawing closer. Mallika moves from the window to where Ambika is sitting.

Ma, tell him to go away. I don't want any undesirable situation to develop here at this time. You're not well, and I don't want anything to happen that might have an adverse effect on your condition.

When Mallika shakes her, Ambika reacts as though she has lost all power of mobility. Her brow is furrowed, and her eyes stare ahead without blinking. The sound of hooves draws very close. Mallika goes back to stand next to Vilom.

Arya Vilom, I've told you to go away. You don't know that . . .

*Having drawn very close, the sound of hooves begins
to recede. Mallika comes to a standstill, as though
paralysed. Vilom turns slightly to look at her.*

VILOM: I'll leave.

A low sarcastic sound escapes his lips.

I don't want to be the cause of any undesirable situation that
might develop here. But may I know—what undesirable
situation could arise?

He moves from the window to the centre of the room.

Well, Ambika, what undesirable situation could arise
because of my presence here?

AMBIKA: I knew it. I've known it ever since he left. If he'd come,
I'd have been surprised. Now, I'm not surprised.

*Her voice grows more shrill. Mallika sits down on
the window seat very slowly, as though she has lost
her strength.*

Not surprised at all. I'm delighted that I was right about
him. Life's only pure emotion! Tender emotion! Very, very
tender emotion!

VILOM: But I'm sorry. I've waited for this day for years. I also
had faith in our friendship . . .

He gives Mallika a meaningful look.

Now, however, that trust is gone. Maybe the friendship
was merely one-sided. He never thought us worthy of his
friendship. And, then, friendship occurs only between like
and like.

*Mallika stands up abruptly. Her eyes are glistening
with the harshness of despair.*

MALLIKA: Arya Vilom!

Vilom looks at her as though he is toying with a child.

I'm telling you again that you should leave. Otherwise,
we'll really have an undesirable situation on our hands.

VILOM: Is that so . . . ?

He looks at Ambika with a smile.

Then I should certainly leave. . . . Okay, Ambika! I worry
a great deal about your health. So far as possible, please
include ghee and honey in your diet. I've extracted some
fresh honey recently. If you need some, I'll send it. . . .

MALLIKA: We don't need any honey. Our home has all the honey
we need.

VILOM: Is that so? . . . Okay, Ambika!

*He looks at both of them for a moment, then walks
away, but pauses at the door.*

. . . but if you do ever need any honey, don't hesitate to ask.

*He leaves. Mallika stands subdued for a moment, with
her head bowed. Unable to collect herself, she moves
towards the inner room. Ambika's expression changes
from anger to hopelessness, and from hopelessness to
compassion.*

AMBIKA: Mallika!

Mallika stops. But she hides her face in her hands without answering. Ambika rises, walks slowly towards her, and takes her in her arms. Mallika buries her face in Ambika's shoulder. Her whole body trembles with grief, but no sound escapes from her lips. Ambika's eyes brim with tears; holding Mallika's trembling frame close to herself, Ambika strokes her back soothingly. Then she begins to kiss the top of Mallika's head, and to rub her cheeks against it, affectionately.

You still want to weep? For that man? For that man who . . . ?

MALLIKA: Don't say anything about him, Ma, don't say anything. . . .

She breaks into sobs. Ambika helps her sit down on the floor right there, and bends over her shaking back.

End of Act Two

Act Three

After some more years.

The sound of rain and thunder. The curtain rises to reveal the same room. One lamp is lit. There is a great difference between the room's condition now and what it was earlier. Everything is decrepit and in disarray. There is only one large jar left, and it is broken at the edge. The window seat has been moved from its old position, and the tiger skin is no longer on it. The decorations painted on the walls, such as the swastikas, are barely visible. There are only one or two blackened pots near the stove. Soiled and tattered clothes are piled up in a corner. Initially, there is no one in the room. Then Matul enters, in wet clothes and walking with a crutch. Looking all around, he sighs deeply and shakes his head in dismay. Then he moves to the middle of the room.

MATUL: Mallika!

Mallika's voice is heard from the inner room.

MALLIKA: Who is it?

MATUL: It's me, Matul. Look at what the rain has done to Matul!

He begins to brush the water off his head and to squeeze it out of his clothes. Mallika emerges from the inner room. Her clothes are torn in places, her complexion has darkened, and the expression in her eyes is a little strange. Her personality shows the same kind of deterioration as the room itself. The portion of the inner room that is visible when the door is open now contains a rickety crib, instead of a bed. Mallika shuts the door behind her.

MALLIKA: Arya Matul—you, here, in this rain?

MATUL: I had no refuge except your home, to escape from this rain. I thought that, no matter what, for Matul you're the same Mallika. . . . This monsoon rain will be the death of me! In the old days, when I could walk on two legs, I never worried about the rain, even the heaviest rain. But now the situation's awful—when I put my crutch forward, my foot slips backwards, and when I put my foot forward, my crutch slips backwards. If I'd known that I'd break my leg in the royal palace, I'd never have left the village at all. And, in my absence, those people turned my house into the kind of place where my feet slip all the time. Compared to the polished marble slabs I have now, my old clay floor was better, because at least it could grip my feet. Now I'm becoming homeless while I still have a home—I can't make it work either inside or outside. Just the sight of those white marble flagstones reminds me of the palace. Where I broke one of my legs!

MALLIKA: It will be hard for you to stand. Please sit down.

Matul goes to the window seat, puts down his crutch,
and settles down, as though for good.

MATUL: If anyone were to ask me, I'd say that there can't be
a more harrowing situation in the world than living in a
palace. If you look in front, you see guards walking ahead
of you. If you look back, you see guards walking towards
you. To tell the truth, I could never figure out whether the
guards were following me or I was following the guards.
. . . And what was even more painful—the very people to
whom I wanted to bow respectfully would, instead, bow
to me. Bow to me . . . ?

He gestures towards himself.

Tell me, what is there in Matul before which anyone should
bow his head? Matul's neither goddess nor god, neither
priest nor king. Then why should anyone bow to Matul
and worship him? But, no—people were ready to worship
not only Matul, but even the clothes that came off his back!
And I used to touch my limbs again and again to check
whether my body was still a thing of flesh and blood, or
whether it had turned into the kind of smooth stone that
one finds in the images of gods and goddesses in temples.
. . . Since I came back here, my greatest joy has been that
no one bows to worship me, and I don't have doubts about
whether I'm the one walking in front, or whether there
are guards walking ahead of me. The only thing I can't
bear is this rain.

MALLIKA: Shall I light a fire to dry out your clothes?

Matul looks first at the stove, then all around him.

MATUL: What a state you've allowed your home to fall into!
Now that Ambika's no more, the house isn't in its proper
condition. . . . Is it true that Priyangumanjari sent you some
clothes and gold jewellery that you refused to accept?

MALLIKA: I didn't need them.

*She walks over to the pile of dirty clothes, pulls out
the blank book from underneath, and begins to dust
it off.*

MATUL: And she had also told the builders to renovate this
house.

MALLIKA: I didn't think any renovation was necessary.

*She looks around for a place to keep the book. Then she
puts it down near Matul on the window seat.*

Let me light a fire.

MATUL: No, the rain's stopping now.

Taking up his crutch, he walks over to the window.

It's only a light drizzle. If I can somehow drag myself
home, I'll dry my clothes there. If the rain starts pouring
down again, then . . .

*Moving away from the window, he draws close to
Mallika.*

Have you heard any news of Kashmir?

She gives him a fixed and sombre look.

MALLIKA: I stay at home all the time. How can I receive any
news from anywhere?

MATUL: I've heard the news. I can't believe it—but, then, I also can. Nothing's impossible in politics. If it's impossible for such-and-such thing to happen, then it's just as possible for the same thing to happen. And it's also perfectly possible that what happens doesn't happen. . . .

Mallika continues looking at him dazedly.

MALLIKA: But what's the news?

MATUL: The news is that the king has passed away. Rebel powers are rearing their heads in Kashmir. A wounded soldier who returned from there says that . . . that Kalidas has left Kashmir.

MALLIKA: He has left Kashmir?

She sits down on the window seat as though she were still in a daze.

And he has gone back now to Ujjayini?

MATUL: No. He hasn't gone back to Ujjayini. The people of the capital city say that he has renounced everything, and has gone off to Kashi. But I don't believe it. He's so well respected in the city. If it wasn't possible for him to stay on in Kashmir, then he ought to have gone straight to the capital. But it isn't impossible, either. There's the life of politics—and then there's Kalidas! To this day, I haven't been able to figure out around what axis either of them turns. I believe the truth's always the exact opposite of whatever I'm able to grasp. And whenever I begin to arrive at the opposite, the truth flips into the opposite of that opposite. That's why, whatever I'm able to grasp is always untrue. From this, you can draw your own conclusion now, about what the truth is—whether he has renounced the world or whether he hasn't. My understanding is that he hasn't renounced the world—so the truth must be that he has, indeed, renounced everything, and has gone off to Kashi.

Mallika picks up the blank book next to her and clutches it to her breast.

MALLIKA: No, that can't be the truth. My heart doesn't accept it.

MATUL: What did I tell you? Whatever I say can never be the truth! That's why I say nothing. If he has gone to Kashi, then I'm lying. If he hasn't gone to Kashi, then, too, I'm lying. . . . Does that satisfy you?

Matul leaves in a huff, banging his crutch noisily. Mallika remains on the window seat, seemingly lost in thought.

MALLIKA: No, you haven't gone off to Kashi. You haven't renounced the world. That's not why I told you to leave this village. . . . I also didn't ask you to leave so that you could go and take on the burden of governance somewhere. When you did so, all the same, I still offered you my best wishes—even though you didn't accept them in person.

She looks at the blank book in her hands, as though with accusation in her eyes.

Even though I didn't remain in your life, you've always been an enduring part of my life. I never let you grow distant from me. You went on creating, and I continued to think that I was meaningful—that my life, too, has accomplished something.

She puts the book down on her knee.

And today, will you reduce my life to meaninglessness in this way?

Placing the book on the seat, she gazes at it with fear, anxiety, and dejection.

You may be detached from life, but I can't be detached from it now. Can you look at life with my eyes? Do you know how these years of my life have been spent? What I've been witness to? What I was, and what I've become?

She rises and throws open the door to the inner room and gestures towards the crib.

Can you see this little creature? Can you recognize her? This is Mallika, who's growing up day by day, and, in place of Ma, I'm the one who's taking care of her now. . . . She's the child of my desolation. No one else could be the fullness, the feeling, that you were in me, but this womb of emptiness contains so many, many images of someone else! Do you know—I've lost my name and acquired an adjective in its place, and now, in my own eyes, I'm not a name but just an adjective.

Shutting the door, she walks towards the window seat.

The traders had said there is gossip in Ujjayini—that you spend a lot of your time in the company of courtesans. . . . But have you seen *this* face of the courtesan? Can you recognize me today? I go to the mountain peak even now and look at the garlands of clouds, just as before. I read lines from *A Gathering of Seasons* and *The Cloud-Messenger*, just as before. I haven't allowed the womb of my emotion to become barren. But can you measure the pain of my deprivation?

She sits down on the floor, with her elbows on the seat,
and picks up the blank book.

No, you can't measure it. You once wrote that a single flaw hides itself in a crowd of virtues, just as the moon's blemish hides itself in a multitude of rays—but destitution can't hide itself. It can't hide itself even in a hundred good qualities. Not only can it not hide, it overshadows a hundred good qualities—destroys them, one by one.

As she speaks, she grows more deeply introspective.

But I endured all this. Because, even as I was breaking, I felt that you were making yourself. Because I saw myself, not in my own self, but in you. And today I hear that you're giving all this up, and renouncing the world? That you're detaching yourself from everyone and everything? Becoming indifferent? Is this how you're going to deprive me of my sense of power?

Lightning flashes, and the sound of thunder can be
heard.

It's a day in the season of rain, just as before. The thunder's rolling, just as before. It's raining, just as before. I'm the same, as before. In the same house, as before. But . . .

*Lightning flashes again and there are more sounds of
thunder. The front door opens, slowly. Kalidas, with
a look of devastation about him, opens the door and
remains standing in the entranceway. In response to
the sound of the door, Mallika looks towards it, and
stands up abruptly. Kalidas enters the room. Mallika
stares at him numbly.*

KALIDAS: Perhaps you don't recognize me.

*Mallika continues to stare at him in the same way.
Kalidas surveys the room, then looks Mallika up and
down, and walks over to the window seat.*

And it's perfectly natural for you not to recognize me,
because I'm not the person you've known in the past. I'm
someone else.

*He sits down on the window seat and leans back on
his arms.*

And, to tell the truth, I'm a person I myself don't recognize!
. . . Why are you standing transfixed like this? Are you very
surprised to see me?

*Mallika shuts the front door, and advances distractedly
towards him.*

MALLIKA: Surprised? I can't believe that you're you—and that
this me, who's watching you, is really me!

KALIDAS: I can see that you, too, aren't the same. Everything has
changed. Or, it's possible that the change has taken place
only in my vision.

MALLIKA: I can't believe that this isn't a dream . . .

KALIDAS: No, it isn't a dream. The reality is that I'm here. After a journey lasting many days, I've arrived here—exhausted, broken, and defeated—to experience the reality of this place once more.

MALLIKA: You're soaking wet. I don't have any dry clothes for you, but I . . .

KALIDAS: Don't worry about my being wet. . . . Do you know, to get wet in the rain like this can also be an ambition in life? It has been years since I got drenched. I don't want to dry off as yet. The walking had tired me out. For several days I was running a fever. But it's as though this rain has taken away all my weariness. . . .

Mallika draws closer to him.

MALLIKA: Are you very tired?

KALIDAS: I was tired. I still need to rest, but the rain has lessened the exhaustion.

MALLIKA: You're really unrecognizable.

Kalidas looks at her for a moment, then gets up and goes to the window.

KALIDAS: And who could recognize you, either? How this house, too, has changed! And I was hoping that everything would be the same—exactly as it was, in its place . . . But nothing's in its proper place.

He looks all around.

You've changed everything. Every single thing.

MALLIKA: I'm not the one who has made the change.

Kalidas looks at her, then begins to walk about.

KALIDAS: I know you haven't made the change. But, Mallika . . .

He comes close to her.

. . . I didn't think this house would ever seem unfamiliar to me. The position and arrangement of every object in it was so settled. But, today, everything seems strange, and . . .

He looks into her eyes.

. . . and, even you. You, too, seem unfamiliar. That's why I say it's possible that the scene hasn't changed as much as my vision has.

MALLIKA: You're tired—sit down. From the look of your eyes it seems that you're still not well.

KALIDAS: I've arrived here after many days of wandering from place to place. The reason why I didn't visit you when I was on my way to Kashmir is exactly the reason I'm visiting you today.

For a moment their gazes meet and lock.

MALLIKA: I learnt from Arya Matul a short while ago that you'd left Kashmir.

KALIDAS: Yes, because my desire for power and status has left me. Today, I'm free of everything that has constricted me for years. In Kashmir, people think I've renounced the world. But I haven't renounced the world. I've only liberated myself from the persona of Matrugupta, so that I may live in the persona of Kalidas again. There was always an attraction pulling me towards the connection I broke off when I left this place. After my departure, I couldn't find anywhere else the intimacy I'd known with each and every thing here. I remember exactly the form and shape of every object here.

He looks around the room once more.

Jars, tiger skin, reed mats, clay lamps, wall decorations . . . and your eyes. What I'd seen of your eyes the day I left is still etched in my memory, to this day. I've been convincing myself all this while that, whenever I return, everything here will be exactly the same as before.

Someone knocks on the door. Taken aback, Mallika looks towards the entranceway. Kalidas wants to go towards the door, but she stops him.

MALLIKA: Don't open the door. Just go on with what you're saying.

KALIDAS: At least go and see who it is.

MALLIKA: It's a rainy day. It could be anybody. You go on talking. He'll go away.

The person at the door turns away, cursing in a drunken voice . . .

'. . . The door's always shut . . . *hunh* . . . the door's always shut!'

KALIDAS: Who was that?

MALLIKA: I told you, it could be anybody. Anyone might need shelter in the rain.

KALIDAS: But I found his voice very strange.

MALLIKA: You were talking about this place.

KALIDAS: I felt as though I knew the voice. As though, like all the other things here, it is also the altered form of some familiar thing.

MALLIKA: You're tired and unwell. Sit down and talk.

Kalidas sighs and sits down on the window seat. Mallika sits down on the floor at a little distance from him, with her arms resting on her knees.

KALIDAS: I've thought many times about myself, Mallika, and every time I've come to the conclusion that Ambika was right.

He stretches his arms behind him, and raises his eyes to the ceiling.

Why didn't I want to leave this place? One reason was that I had no confidence in myself. I didn't know how I would feel in an environment of fame and honour, after living a life of deprivation and abuse. Somewhere in my mind was the anxiety that such an environment would overwhelm me, and change my life's direction. . . . And that anxiety wasn't quite baseless.

His eyes turn towards Mallika.

You were very surprised that I was going to take up the governorship of Kashmir, weren't you? You must have found that very unnatural. But none of it seems unnatural to me. It was a natural reaction to a life of deprivation.

Quite possibly, my reaction also contained a desire for revenge against all the people who'd abused me at will, who'd made me a laughing stock.

Biting his lip, he gets up abruptly and goes to the window.

But I also knew that I couldn't be happy. I tried to convince myself over and over again that the source of this shortcoming wasn't my environment, but my own self. If I could change myself, I'd be happy. But that didn't happen. I could neither change nor be happy. I was granted power and authority, I was given a great deal of honour, manuscript copies of whatever I wrote reached every corner of the country—but I couldn't find happiness. That environment and that way of life might have been natural for someone else, but they weren't for me. My field of action was different from a royal official's field of action. I felt over and over again that, by falling into the temptations of lordship and convenience, I'd entered that sphere illegitimately, and that I was far removed from the terrain on which I should have stayed. Whenever my gaze fell upon the horizon stretching far into the distance, I was pained by the perception that I'd removed myself from my own proper domain. I'd reassure myself that one day—tomorrow, if not today—I'd establish control over my circumstances, and divide myself equally between the two fields of action. But I continued to be moulded and driven by my circumstances. The tomorrow for which I was waiting never arrived, and I went on breaking, breaking, into pieces. And, one day . . . one day, I discovered that I was completely broken. I wasn't the person who was connected in any way to that large domain.

He falls silent for a moment. Then he resumes walking about.

I didn't want to pass through this place on my way to Kashmir. I felt at the time that this region, this range of mountains and valleys, would take the form of a mute question before me. Still, I couldn't resist the temptation. But I didn't experience any joy in being here. I was repelled by myself. I was also repelled by all those people who celebrated the day of my visit with festivities. That was the first time my heart and mind longed to be liberated. But it wasn't possible to be liberated then. I didn't visit you that day because I was afraid your eyes would make my restless heart even more restless. I wanted to save myself from such a situation. It could have had any kind of consequence. I knew what effect my failure to visit you would have on you, what others would say to you. Even so, I felt reassured that you wouldn't have any negative feelings in that respect. And I left with the hope that there would come a day when I'd be able to say all this to you, and convince you about the conflicts in my mind. . . . I didn't realize that conflict doesn't limit itself to just one person, that change doesn't move only in one direction. That's why I've a great sense of futility about being here today.

He goes back to the window.

People think I've written a lot while living that life and being in that environment. But I know I haven't written anything while living there. Whatever I've written was only the cumulative effect of my life here. These Himalaya mountains are the background of *The Origin of the Young God*, and the ascetic goddess Uma is you. The anguish of the imprisoned demigod in *The Cloud-Messenger* is my anguish, and his wife, stricken by the grief of separation from him, is you—even though I've imagined myself trapped on a mountain peak here, and envisioned you living in the city. In my play *The Recognition of Shakuntala*, you were the one who stood before me in the form of Shakuntala. Whenever I tried to write, I repeated the history of your life and mine, again and again. And whenever I sought to write at a distance from that history, my work didn't spring to life. The lamentation of Aja in my epic, *Raghu's Dynasty*, is nothing but a representation of my own pain, and . . .

Mallika hides her face in her hands. Kalidas stops speaking suddenly, and stares at her for a moment.

I wanted you to be able to read all this, but the connecting thread broke in such a way that . . .

Removing her hands from her face, Mallika shakes her head in disagreement.

MALLIKA: The connecting thread never broke.

She picks up the manuscript pages wrapped in cloth, and places them in Kalidas's hands. Kalidas looks through the pages.

KALIDAS: *The Cloud-Messenger*! How did a copy of *The Cloud-Messenger* reach you?

MALLIKA: I have all your works. I was able to get copies of *Raghu's Dynasty* and *The Recognition of Shakuntala* just a few months ago.

KALIDAS: You have all my works? But how did they become available here? Did . . . ?

MALLIKA: The merchants of Ujjayini sometimes travel along this route, too.

KALIDAS: And you can get these manuscript copies from them?

MALLIKA: I asked them specially to get the copies for me. Each time it took a year or two to find a copy somewhere.

KALIDAS: And the money to pay for them?

MALLIKA: It took a year or two to get a copy. There was plenty of time to save up the money.

> *Kalidas sits down on the window seat with his head bowed.*

KALIDAS: The deprivations that have gnawed at me for years look even larger today, Mallika! I should have returned to this place years ago, so that I could get soaked in the rain, and then write—write everything that I haven't been able to write so far, and that has been gathering inside me for years like clouds in the season of rain . . .

> *Sighing deeply, he picks up the blank book lying on the seat, and begins to turn its pages.*

. . . but is unable to come down as rain. Because it can't find its proper season. It can't find the right wind . . . What poem is this? These are merely blank pages!

MALLIKA: I made these bark pages with my own hands and stitched them together. I thought that when you came visiting from the capital, I'd give you this blank book as a gift. That I'd say, 'Compose your greatest epic on these pages.' But, even when you visited once, you chose not to visit, and this gift simply lay around here. Now these pages are beginning to fall apart, and I feel hesitant to say that they're for you to write on.

Kalidas keeps turning the pages.

KALIDAS: You made these pages with your own hands so that I may write my epic on them!

Turning the pages, he pauses at one place in the bound volume.

Drops of water have fallen on the pages in various places, but there's no doubt that they weren't drops of rain. It seems that you've written a great deal on these blank sheets with your eyes. And not just with your eyes—in some places, the pages are soiled with beads of sweat, in other places, dry flower petals have left traces of their colour. In many places, your nails have peeled off their layers, your teeth have bitten them apart. And, in addition to these marks, the fading and discolouration caused by the summer sun, the dust of crumbling winter leaves, and the dampness of this house . . . In what sense are these pages blank any more, Mallika? An epic has already been composed on them—an epic with an infinite number of cantos.

He puts down the volume.

What new writing can be done on these pages now?

Rising, he goes to the window. He looks out for a few moments, then turns back towards Mallika.

But there's life still ahead of us. We can begin again from the beginning.

The sound of a baby crying and whimpering is heard from the inner room. Mallika gets up quickly and walks towards it, visibly anxious and perturbed. Kalidas watches her go, looking as though he were stunned.

KALIDAS: Mallika!

Mallika pauses, and looks at him.

Who's crying?

MALLIKA: This is my present—my here and now.

She goes inside. Kalidas comes and stands in the middle of the room, as though he were frozen.

KALIDAS: Your present?

Someone knocks on the front door, then kicks it open. Vilom appears in the entranceway, cursing at the door. His clothes are muddy. He enters, swaying a little.

VILOM: On a wet day, brother Vilom, you've slipped and fallen, and fallen straight into a ditch. . . . I've told you so often, don't ever climb up too high. But why would brother Vilom listen? When he first came, the door was shut. He went away and slipped and fell. He came back, and the door was shut. And suppose he'd gone away again? Today is the kind of day when . . .

Seeing Kalidas, he stops mid-sentence. He looks like
someone examining a minute object very carefully.

Who knows what's happened to these eyes of mine?
Sometimes unfamiliar figures look very familiar, and
sometimes even familiar figures don't look familiar . . .
Now, this is a very familiar figure, but I just can't recognize
it. I know this figure well, but the personality seems new
. . . Hey, brother, do you know me?

Mallika emerges from the interior and, catching sight
of Vilom, freezes at the door of the inner room.

KALIDAS: Your appearance has changed a lot, but you're still the
same person today.

VILOM: I'm acquainted with this voice, and also these words.

He tries to fix his eyes upon Kalidas, and to look closely.
Then he suddenly bursts into laughter.

So, it's you—you? . . . All my troubles from falling and
hurting myself have vanished! I've had such a desire to set
my eyes upon you, for so long. Come . . .

He opens his arms towards Kalidas, but the latter
moves away.

You won't embrace me? Because my body is soiled? Or do
you just detest me? But the connection between you and
me can't be broken off so easily. You'd said, hadn't you,
that we're very close to each other. Didn't you say that?
In all these years I haven't let any distance creep into our
closeness. In fact, I believe that we're even closer now.

He turns towards Mallika.

Why, Mallika, am I not right? . . . Why are you standing there as though you are frozen? Vilom's no longer an uninvited guest in this home. Now he enters it by right. No? Now he can welcome Kalidas, and offer him hospitality in this house. No?

He turns to Kalidas again.

You'll say how much of a matter of chance this is—that we met in this house back then, and that we're meeting here again today. But, believe me, it isn't a matter of chance. Whenever you would have come to visit, this is where we would have met.

He turns towards Mallika once more.

You haven't yet begun the formalities of welcoming Kalidas as a guest? To have a guest in your home after years and to not welcome him properly? Do you know—know how much Kalidas loves the fawns of this region . . . ?

He turns back towards Kalidas.

There's a little fawn in this house, too . . . Haven't you seen Mallika's little girl? Her eyes are no less beautiful than a fawn's. And do you know what Ashtavakra says? He says . . .

Mallika steps forward quickly.

MALLIKA: Arya Vilom!

Vilom laughs.

VILOM: You don't want Kalidas to know what Ashtavakra says!

But I'm not convinced by his observation. That's why I was about to say, it's possible that Kalidas may be able to look and tell how far Ashtavakra is right. Do the little girl's features really resemble Vilom's features, or . . . ?

Hiding her face in her hands, Mallika goes to the window seat and sits down. Vilom moves close to Kalidas.

Come—will you look?

KALIDAS: Go away from here, Vilom!

VILOM: Go away?

He laughs.

From this house, or from the province itself? I've heard that governance is a very mighty business. There's a great deal of power and privilege in lordship.

KALIDAS: I'm telling you that right now you should leave.

VILOM: Just because you've come back? . . . Because the land you left many years ago seems to be yours again today? . . . Because your rights are perpetual?

He laughs.

You talk as though life has no motion, no vitality, outside you. All that exists is you—there's no one else. But time isn't heartless. It has empowered others, too. Has given them rights. Time didn't stop short on the threshold of this house, bearing oblations of incense and food without actually offering them. It has given others opportunity! It has built something. . . . Are you repelled by what time has built? Because you can't see yourself where you wanted to see yourself?

Vilom stares at Kalidas for several moments, and laughs again.

You want me to leave immediately. I'll leave. Not because you're ordering me to leave. Only because you're a guest here today, and a guest's wish must be honoured.

He walks towards the front door, but pauses near it and looks back at Mallika.

Make sure, Mallika, that nothing's lacking in our hospitality. We don't know whether a guest who's visiting us for the first time in many years will ever come back.

He gives both Mallika and Kalidas a meaningful look and leaves. Mallika uncovers her face and looks at Kalidas. Both remain silent for a few moments.

MALLIKA: What are you thinking about?

Kalidas walks over to the window.

KALIDAS: I'm thinking that that was a day in the season of rain exactly like this one. Clouds were amassed in the valley exactly like this, and an untimely darkness had set in. I had seen a wounded fawn in the valley, and picked it up and brought it here. You had attended to it.

Mallika gets up and goes near him.

MALLIKA: You're thinking about something else, too!

KALIDAS: And I'm thinking that the expanse of lowlands at the foot of the mountains is still the same. The path that leads to the mountain peak is also the same. The moisture in the wind is as it was before. The sounds in the environment are also as they were before.

MALLIKA: And?

KALIDAS: And that it's the same pulsating consciousness within me. The same heart that surges with emotion. But . . .

Mallika looks at him in silence. Kalidas moves from the window to the seat, where he picks up the blank book.

. . . but, at that time, this epic of blank pages hadn't been written yet.

MALLIKA: You were saying that you want to begin again at the beginning.

Kalidas sighs.

KALIDAS: I said that I want to begin from the beginning. Perhaps it was a confrontation between desire and time. But I see that time is more powerful, because . . .

MALLIKA: Because?

The baby's crying is audible from the interior once more. Mallika rushes into the inner room. Kalidas puts down the volume on the seat and speaks as though he were answering her question, but only to himself.

KALIDAS: Because time doesn't wait.

Lightning flashes, and the sound of thunder is heard. Kalidas looks all around once and goes to the window. It begins to rain. Returning to the seat, he picks up the blank book and looks at it one more time, then sets it down again. He casts a glance towards the inner room, then goes to the entranceway. He pauses there for a moment, as though lost in thought. Then he leaves, and shuts the front door behind him. The sound of thunder and rain increases. After a few moments, Mallika emerges from the inner room, holding the baby close to her breast. Not seeing Kalidas, she runs to the window.

MALLIKA: Kalidas!

Still clutching the baby, she goes from the window to the entranceway, and throws open the front door.

Kalidas!

She begins to move towards the threshold, but, looking at the child in her arms, comes to a dead stop. As though broken in spirit, she goes to the window seat and sits down. Hugging the child even closer to herself, she begins to weep as she kisses it. Lightning flashes again and again, and the thunder continues to roll.

The End

Afterword

VINAY DHARWADKER

Self-reflexivity is not exclusive to modernism, but modernist aesthetic practice is self-reflexive in most forms, even though the kind and the degree of self-consciousness it displays vary over time and space, and diversify across genres, arts, and cultures. A modernist writer and an innovator of the first order, Mohan Rakesh weaves two main types of self-referential discourse into the fabric of *Ashadh ka ek din*, which diverge in their functions even as they integrate the overall dramatic design with plot, character, and dialogue in the text and with the mise en scène in performance. Like their counterparts in other modernist works—from Joseph Conrad's 'I' in the outer frame of *Heart of Darkness* (1900) and T.S. Eliot's notes to *The Waste Land* (1922), to Gertrude Stein's third-person self-narrative in *The Autobiography of Alice B. Toklas* (1933) and Orson Welles' snow globe in *Citizen Kane* (1941)—Rakesh's moments of authorial intervention have the potential to fundamentally transform our understanding of the play.

Although audiences spanning several generations have read, watched, and responded to *Ashadh* for more than fifty years, for the most part they have overlooked the intricacy of its self-reflexive modernism. In the years following its initial editions and productions in the late 1950s and early 1960s, Rakesh expanded on his intentions, aesthetics, craft, and theory of drama and theatre on a number of occasions, but his vocabulary of plotted narrative and symbolic representation (*kathanak* and *pratik*, respectively) allowed him to explicate the play's structure and technique with limited success. In an exchange reported in 1996—almost a quarter-century after Rakesh's death—scholar Jaidev Taneja and actor-director Ramgopal Bajaj pinpointed the most important self-referential segment in the text, but they did not have the means to name or analyse its components, noting wishfully that 'the day a director or an actor . . . succeeds in bringing it fully to life on stage . . . the real meaning of *Ashadh* will reveal itself, and the play will receive the assessment it deserves'.[1] For Rakesh and his immediate contemporaries, the difficulty was that almost all the theories capable of explaining the play either appeared in the international community of scholars after it was written in 1958, or began to circulate in academic networks a decade later, and hence were unavailable during the formative debates in India. For others, the continuing handicap has been that the necessary critical concepts have spread widely since the 1970s, but have filtered rather slowly into the discussion of Indian drama, and no one so far has risked applying them to Rakesh's extraordinary inventions in the play.

The two primary configurations of self-reflexive discourse in *Ashadh* come from Rakesh's repertoire of devices as a writer and a modernist. In my analysis below, the first of these devices creates several 'reflections' in the text that multiply its meanings, change the thrust of its narrative, and complicate the connections between 'the fictional Kalidas' and 'the historical Kalidas', even as they amplify the characters and expand the structure of the play. In contrast, the second device inserts novelistic discourse into the dramatic action and the mise en scène, which reverses the conventional relation between enactment and language, or 'showing' and 'telling', in the theatre and on the page; at the same time, it redefines the genre of the play and unsettles the setting of its action. Both techniques contribute directly to Rakesh's construction of a particular picture of classical India, to his relations with his classical sources, and to the dialectic of historical precedence and aesthetic innovation that he sets in motion. Viewed as part of a larger ensemble, these dynamic techniques allow us to gauge how Rakesh modernizes the past and classicizes the present simultaneously; and why, especially in his preface to the first edition of *Laharon ke rajhans* (The Royal Swans of the Waves) in 1963, he places both transfigurations inside 'the time of literature' rather than 'the time of history'.[2] Against such a backdrop, this Afterword provides a set of analytical procedures and perspectives for a fresh exploration of *Ashadh*, its interior and exterior relations, its textual constitution and interpretive reconstructions, its multiple filiations and affiliations.

Mirrors in the Text

The Mise en Abyme

Rakesh's principal authorial intervention in *Ashadh* takes the form of a *mise en abyme*—the device that eluded Taneja and Bajaj—and appears in the extended monologue by the fictional Kalidas, at the climax of the play in the middle of Act Three, when he says to Mallika:

> These Himalaya mountains are the background of *The Origin of the Young God*, and the ascetic goddess Uma is you. The anguish of the imprisoned demigod in *The Cloud-Messenger* is my anguish, and his wife, stricken by the grief of separation from him, is you—even though I've imagined myself trapped on a mountain peak here, and envisioned you living in the city. In my play *The Recognition of Shakuntala*, you were the one who stood before me in the form of Shakuntala. Whenever I tried to write, I repeated the history of your life and mine, again and again. And whenever I sought to write at a distance from that history, my work didn't spring to life. The lamentation of Aja in my epic, *Raghu's Dynasty*, is nothing but a representation of my own pain, and . . . [see p. 177]

A literary *mise en abyme* embeds one text inside another, with the smaller, inset text serving as a 'miniature mirror' that reflects the larger text that frames it. More generally, the nested text is metaphorically a microcosm of the work surrounding it, and hence replicates the characteristics, clarifies the meaning, or explains the signification and significance of its macrocosm.[3] André Gide adapts the French term for the analysis of art and literature from the craft of heraldry, where it is used for the 'placement' (*mise*) of a small-scale coat-of-arms 'in the centre' (*en abyme*) of an identical but full-sized coat-of-arms.

The secondary coat is a visual icon of the primary one; by the logic of iconography, it contains (in theory) a reduced image of itself at its centre which, in turn, contains its own miniature at its centre, and so on—an instance of self-reproduction in a geometric series of reductions that run ad infinitum, and hence end up 'in an abyss' (the other meaning of *en abyme*).

As a modernist technique, the *mise en abyme* becomes a defining characteristic of Jorge Luis Borges' *ficciones* after his surrealist experiments in the 1920s and 1930s, for example, and is as central to 'Pierre Menard, Author of the Quixote' (1939) as to 'The Aleph' (1945, rev. 1974).[4] In the former story, a fragment of a sentence from *Don Quixote* serves as 'the mirror in the text' that defines and explains the Frenchman Menard's extreme 'ambition' to achieve '*total* identification with a specific author', especially 'to forget European history between 1602 and 1918', and 'to *be* Miguel de Cervantes' at the height of high modernism; as well as his attempt, growing out of his obsessive identification with the early-modern Spanish author, to write or (re)construct the latter's seminal novel, word for word, without actually copying the original.[5] In the second story, the narrator agrees fearfully but voluntarily to be isolated in his antagonist's cellar, where he gets to see 'an Aleph', which is 'one of the points in space that contains all other points'.[6] Lying on his back on the floor, in 'total darkness, total immobility', he focuses his eyes on the nineteenth step of the cellar stairs, and witnesses, 'On the back part of the step, toward the right, . . . a small iridescent sphere of almost unbearable brilliance':

> The Aleph's diameter was probably little more than an inch, but all space was there, actual and undiminished.

Each thing (a mirror's face, let us say) was infinite things,
since I distinctly saw it from every angle of the universe.
I saw the teeming sea; I saw daybreak and nightfall; I saw
the multitudes of America; I saw a silvery cobweb in the
center of a black pyramid; I saw a splintered labyrinth (it
was London); I saw, close up, unending eyes watching
themselves in me as in a mirror; I saw all the mirrors on
earth. . . . I saw the circulation of my own dark blood; I
saw the coupling of love and the modification of death;
I saw the Aleph from every point and angle, and in the
Aleph I saw the earth and in the earth the Aleph and in
the Aleph the earth. . . .[7]

He weeps, 'for my eyes had seen that secret and conjectured
object whose name is common to all men but which no man
has looked upon—the unimaginable universe'; dizzy and
overcome, he feels 'infinite wonder, infinite pity'.[8] This is a
normative moment in modernism, because Borges' invention
defines the properties of the device in its most general form: a
textual representation of an object that *synecdochically* mirrors,
and hence reveals the meaning of, the whole of which it is a
representative part. It is general because what is invoked here
is not a text but an object—a mathematical object, though
manifested physically as an 'iridescent sphere'—and, through
a variation of Zeno's paradox, it literally contains the infinite
whole of which it is an infinitesimal component, and whose
structure and meaning it therefore paradoxically circumscribes.
By its peculiar logic of infinitude and inexhaustibility
(an 'abyss'), the Aleph is the primordial 'ontological
original' of all possible textual instances of a *mise en abyme*.

The most famous literary example of the device is an early-modern one: the play within the play in William Shakespeare's *Hamlet*, the mirroring effect or explanatory function of which we interpret as 'a *Hamlet* within *Hamlet*'. One of its oldest and most intriguing occurrences in world literature is in the Mahabharata, which contains a condensed but complete retelling of the Ramayana in its *Ramopakhyana* section, set inside its third major book, the *Aranyaka Parvan* (the Book of the Forest). The placement of the *Ramopakhyana* as a scaled mirror inside the Mahabharata enables the microcosmic or summary narrative (Rama's response, in exile, to Ravana's abduction of Sita) to clarify the meaning of its macrocosmic narrative (Yudhishthira's response, in exile, to Jayadratha's abduction of Draupadi).[9] In the classical period, which follows a long period of the epics in India, Kalidas himself famously uses a *mise en abyme* in the interlude preceding the third act of his play, *Vikramorvashiya* (Vikrama and Urvashi; or, Urvashi Won by Valour), which is not mentioned in *Ashadh*. In the Sanskrit text, the celestial nymph Urvashi acts—offstage—in a play within the play, directed for the gods by Bharata, the legendary author of the *Natyashastra* (c. 300 CE), and inadvertently reveals her love affair with the protagonist Pururavas; in the process, she mirrors the way in which Pururavas himself inadvertently reveals his infatuation with her—but to his wife and queen, onstage, with consequences.

Embedded Texts in Ashadh

When Rakesh writes *Ashadh* over a stretch of fifty days in March–April 1958, Borges' fiction is not yet in significant circulation outside the Spanish hemisphere—which happens in the 1960s when, for example, his experiments inspire Michel Foucault's *The Order of Things* (1966); and the device of textual mirroring is not yet a centrepiece of Euro-American post-structuralism and postmodernism— which happens after Jacques Derrida's discussion of Stephen Mallarmé in *Dissemination* (1972). It is therefore likely that Rakesh, drawing on Kalidas and Shakespeare, possibly on the Mahabharata, and on other premodern sources (such as the *One Thousand and One Nights*), produces a modernist version of the device 'from scratch', for himself and on his own; and the structure he invents for it proves to be unique in modern world drama.

Ventriloquizing through his fictional protagonist, Rakesh interpolates his modernist play with miniature versions of *four* works conventionally ascribed to the classical Sanskrit poet: *Kumara-sambhava* (The Origin of the Young God), a long poem that survives incomplete in ten cantos; *Meghaduta* (The Cloud-Messenger), an extended lyrical envoi of more than 110 verses; *Abhijnana-shakuntala* (The Recognition of Shakuntala), a full-length play based on a traditional story, in seven acts; and *Raghuvamsha* (Raghu's Dynasty), a court epic in nineteen cantos that we have inherited possibly in an unfinished state.[10] He then explicitly and implicitly identifies the inset Sanskrit texts with elements in *Ashadh* on five distinct planes: he identifies Mallika with the various heroines of the classical works; the fictional Kalidas with the corresponding protagonists; his invented modernist story of the Mallika– Kalidas relationship with the stories of their four counterparts in Sanskrit; *Ashadh* as a whole with the historical poet's works; and himself, as a modern writer, with the Kalidas postulated to have lived around the turn of the fifth century. Each of the identifications in the array, however, turns out to have a complicated structure, and hence transmogrifies any interpretation of the play that we may have constructed before encountering this segment in Act Three.

The effect of this *mise en abyme* on Mallika is to split up her character and her individual story into four mirror images in Sanskrit literature or, conversely, to roll four classical representations of women into one modern and modernist composite, so that *ethos* and *muthos* now acquire four additional dimensions (Aristotle's terms for character and plot, respectively).[11] The fictive characters with whom Mallika is identified explicitly embody and display aspects of her imagined 'personality' and 'life experience' that have remained latent up to this point in the play. Thus, if Mallika mirrors Uma (the goddess Parvati) in *The Origin of the Young God*, then she is a naive charmer repeatedly rebuffed by an arrogant and insensitive older man (the god Shiva), who deliberately keeps himself out of her reach, and so drives her to extremes of self-mortification (*tapasya*, ascetic discipline) in her fixation with winning his affections and persuading him to propose marriage. If Mallika mirrors the *yakshi* or demigoddess in *The Cloud-Messenger*, then she is a reciprocally passionate beloved left behind by a partner who, unknown to her, has been banished and imprisoned by his master, and is unable to send her the news, while she suffers in isolation at home, agonizing over his absence and silence. If Mallika mirrors Shakuntala in *The Recognition of Shakuntala*, then she is a young wife who has boldly married a man of her choice, but secretly and without parental consent or societal approval;

whose new husband leaves her in order to pursue his worldly engagements, with a promise to send for her soon; and who then discovers that she has been deserted and has to survive on her own as a single mother, without material assistance from either her natal family or her absconding husband. If Mallika mirrors Indumati, the queen of King Aja (Dasharatha's father and Rama's grandfather) in *Raghu's Dynasty*, then she is a spouse and soulmate who is 'snatched away' from her doting husband at the happiest time of their lives, and whose premature death is an injustice, a perversity inflicted by the gods.

Parallel to the de-composition and re-composition of Mallika, the consequence of the quadrilateral 'mirror' in the text for the fictional Kalidas also is to divide him into, or constitute him as an amalgam of, four fictive characters. Thus, Rakesh's protagonist is callous and self-centred, but commits later in the narrative to unconditional love and lifelong faithfulness (like Lord Shiva in *The Origin of the Young God*); he is an absent, passionate partner who wants to communicate his longing, but whose circumstances prevent him from doing so (the *yaksha* in *The Cloud-Messenger*); he is a secret husband who leaves and 'forgets' his wife initially, but 'remembers' her subsequently and is overcome by guilt and remorse, which lead him back to her, to seek a fresh start (Dushyanta in *The Recognition of Shakuntala*); and he is an adoring husband who grieves inconsolably for a wife he has lost to the gods' unfathomable cruelty (Aja in *Raghu's Dynasty*).

Once established, each of these mirrored elaborations of the characters of Mallika and Kalidas expands and modifies the scope of their relationship, until its fabric has been completely changed. In Act One, when they part for the first time, they are still young and idealistic lovers outside marriage, and, in spite of Ambika's scepticism and Vilom's mockery, Mallika still seems to believe—like Shakuntala in relation to Dushyanta—that she can induce her Kalidas to 'recognize' her, and to carry her with him into his new life as a courtier. By the end of Act Three, however, their combined fictional life stories have passed through separation, unrequited love, desertion, unfaithfulness, promiscuity, prostitution, single motherhood, abuse and violence (at the hands of others), repeated abandonment, and an irreversible final 'divorce'. In the course of a dozen concatenated scenes, which are not differentiated formally in the text, Mallika and Kalidas multiply into several pairs of lovers, and the tale of their one relationship becomes the cumulative story of many couples at once. Following the same logic as in Borges' 'The Aleph' but on a diminished scale, Rakesh's *mise en abyme* thus invests *Ashadh* with an inner structure that multiplies elements like images in mirrors facing each other, producing a regress of simulacrum upon simulacrum, Chinese box within Chinese box.

The Doppelgänger

The specific method used by Borges and Rakesh is part of a hierarchy of aesthetic devices in literature, in which the most general technique is repetition. As A.K. Ramanujan notes in his essay on the Mahabharata (1988),

> repetition or replication is the central principle of any structuring. What occurs only once does not allow us to

talk of structure. *Einmal ist keinmal*—it's as if what happens
once doesn't happen at all.[12]

'Indian artworks,' Ramanujan continues, 'are built on the
principle of interacting structures of repetition and elaboration
and variation.' Repetition occurs in the visual and verbal arts in
several distinct forms, one of which involves its application on
a limited scale in the process of 'doubling'. While expounding
on Derrida's treatment of 'replications', Marian Hobson
observes that 'mirrors create doubles'; 'with the *mise en abyme*
as a series of reflections on internally contained scale-models
of the literary work, such doubles might give consistency
and coherence' to the containing text 'by encapsulating
images which reflect the whole, by reinforcing and repeating
it'.[13] If, for a moment, we view Rakesh's devices through the
twin wide-angle lenses provided by Ramanujan and Derrida,
then *Ashadh* appears as a whole that is 'reflexive' in itself,
that actively 'reflects' its structure, and that contains its own
'reflection'; as a self-reflexive structure, it employs a hierarchy
of repetitions; and, since internal textual mirroring is a sub-
variety of doubling, the device in Act Three is affiliated with
other doublings in the text.

Among these is the application of doubling—the technique
of one initial repetition—to a human figure or persona: 'the
mirror which doubles the person looking into it' projects 'the
figure of a subject' or an agent of consciousness and action.[14]
Rakesh employs doubling self-consciously to generate Vilom
as a doppelgänger: paralleling the function of the *mise en
abyme*, this figure appears on stage—near the end of each
act—as an *ethical mirror* in which the other principal characters

can see their 'true reflections', or recognize themselves as moral subjects required to choose and act. In Act One, Vilom interacts with Ambika, Mallika, and Kalidas together; in Act Two, with Ambika and Mallika as a mother–daughter pair, while Kalidas visits the village without visiting them; and, in Act Three, with Mallika and Kalidas as a couple, after Ambika's death and shortly before the poet's final desertion. As Vilom's dialogue in these scenes shows, he is a composite doppelgänger for all three characters, as much Ambika's harsh and combative antagonist as Mallika's or Kalidas's—but he is a darker anti-self for each than, say, Charles Baudelaire's double in *The Flowers of Evil* (1857), invoked ironically as '—*mon semblable,* —*mon frère*' (my kinsman who resembles me, my brother).[15] To use catachresis in a lighter vein, Vilom's 'frictional relationships with his fractional opposites' do not make him a mirror image of each co-respondent, but turn him instead into a mirror *inversion* of each. While the main device of textual self-reflection repeats and reinforces the characters of Mallika and Kalidas by multiplying them, the doppelgänger device embodied in Vilom inverts, subverts, contraverts, and dramatically challenges not only Mallika and Kalidas but also Ambika. If the quadrangular *mise en abyme* in *Ashadh* is a mirror of faithful replications, then Vilom as a doppelgänger is a mirror of inverted, abrasive doubles.

The placement of self-reflections in the text thus unfolds the semantic layers that have accumulated in the dialogue and the stage directions up to the middle of Act Three; and it explains not only the emplotment but also the characters and their imaginary life stories—as much to them, inside the play, as to the audience outside it. The device regulates the figure of Kalidas in *Ashadh*—as he is fictionalized in it, as he relates to 'the historical Kalidas', and as the factual and fictional dimensions of his representation intermesh with the author's, reader's, and viewer's literary–historical imaginations. Moreover, it embodies a more general principle of internal textual replication that connects the configuration in Act Three to subsidiary devices, such as the doppelgänger, which alter the characters' mutual interactions as well as the audience's interpretation of the action as a whole. At the level of artistic practice, it enables Rakesh to ventriloquize through his mirror images of Kalidas (conceived as a *pratik* or 'symbolic representation' in Hindi), and hence transitively through the mirror images of Mallika, to give us a glimpse of what Taneja and Bajaj designate as 'the real meaning of *Ashadh*'. In the process, Rakesh not only functions as a self-reflexive author who 'remains within . . . his handiwork', like James Joyce in *A Portrait of the Artist as a Young Man* (1916), but also metamorphoses the play into a self-reflecting whole, in which various devices, including the doppelgänger, disperse the effects of replication throughout the text until—as W.B. Yeats puts it in 'The Statues'—'Mirror on mirror mirrored is all the show'.[16]

Novelistic Discourse in Drama

Rakesh's second self-reflexive intervention takes the form of an almost interlinear 'novelization' of the dramatic discourse in *Ashadh*, a supplement to the dialogue which, in its historical moment in the late 1950s, pushes textuality to a new modernist limit, and not merely in its postcolonial context. The immediate impact of this device on how readers, spectators, and performers perceive the play is twofold: on the one hand, it changes our perception of how the represented action mixes and manages 'showing' and 'telling' in the text and on the stage; and, on the other, it alters our conventional expectations regarding its fictive time and place, or 'setting'. More so than the comparable devices developed by his modernist counterparts in Europe and the Americas, Rakesh's novelistic interceptions actively influence the staging of *Ashadh*, its reception in performance, and its profile along the spectrum of dramatic genres.

Rakesh's Stage Directions

If the specific structure of the *mise en abyme* in Act Three requires Rakesh to project his commentary on to a fictional character, then his second self-reflexive technique allows him, by contrast, to inject his own voice directly into the text. His device of choice consists of stage directions, which conventionally represent a dramatist's blueprint for the mise en scène—the overall disposition of performers and properties in a stage setting or a physical environment for a theatrical production—in the texture of the verbal artefact.

In the transnational print culture of drama and theatre since early modernity, a play-text is an intercalation of two distinct 'discourses': the *dramatic discourse* of the action itself, containing the dialogue and supplementary material in words (such as lyrics for any songs) to be staged before an audience; and the *dramatist's discourse*, comprising mainly stage directions (which may be inserted also by editors, translators, directors, or dramaturges), together with authorial commentary in other forms attached to the work (such as prefaces, dedications, or notes). In Shakespeare's play scripts, the stage directions are sparse and threadbare, interpolated in a style that resurfaces in Harold Pinter and David Mamet; but with Ben Jonson, and especially after the Restoration playwrights in England, devices such as the author's dedication (often to an aristocratic patron) become increasingly self-reflexive, until Henrik Ibsen, August Strindberg, George Bernard Shaw, and Eugene O'Neill, in the late-nineteenth and the twentieth centuries, transmute the dramatist's discourse into a semi-autonomous art form that is as vital as—and inseparable from—the dramatic discourse itself. The spiralling 'imbalance' between the two components of the play-text reaches its logical limit in some of Samuel Beckett's late-modernist 'shorts', where the complete text for the thirty-five-second-long dramatic action of *Breath*, for instance, consists solely of stage directions, which describe exactly how one 'Faint brief cry' (repeated once) and one inhalation and exhalation (in 'Amplified recording'), without actors in live performance, are to be synchronized with a 'Faint light on stage littered with miscellaneous rubbish'—a refutation of Aristotle's prescription that *melos* and *opsis* (sound and spectacle) are subordinate to the quadrivium of *muthos*, *ethos*, *lexis*, and *dianoia* (plot, characters, diction, and theme, respectively).

Rakesh's device of self-reflexive stage directions in *Ashadh*, which sometimes occur in whole passages (as at the beginning of each act) but which, more importantly, appear at some length on almost every page of the play, aligns him with O'Neill's reflective modernism, rather than with Shaw's garrulous, querulous socialism. William Davies King observes that in O'Neill's *Long Day's Journey into Night* (published in 1956, two years before *Ashadh*),

> The remarkably precise and detailed opening stage directions . . . , which some have criticized as excessive, are meant for readers of the play, not directors, designers, and actors. O'Neill intended for the play to be published twenty-five years after his death but never produced. He aimed to represent context in the way that a novelist does, so that the action could be imagined—seen, heard, felt—from the published script alone. The same goes for the parenthetical line readings . . . , which are meant not to coach actors but to help the reader imagine a performance. Descriptions of the setting and characters provide an exact portrait from memory of O'Neill's home in New London, Connecticut, in August 1912. The directive notes, in contrast, reflect a virtual performance of the play that he has constructed as drama.[17]

Despite his affinity, Rakesh deviates from his older Irish-American contemporary's example to a significant extent: he fully intends *Ashadh* to be a performance vehicle in the present and, as he attests on several occasions, his ideal is a play-text fashioned interactively with directors, performers, and material realities in the theatre. Moreover, in 1958, he already is a successful fiction writer in the *nai kahani* (new story) movement in postcolonial Hindi, and is about to emerge as a notable practitioner of modernist realism in the *naya upanyas* (new novel) movement.[18] While O'Neill's directions and directives in *Long Day's Journey* are only analogous to a novelist's 'way' of representing the 'context' of its action, Rakesh's authorial intervention in his play is fully realized *novelistic discourse* interspersed throughout the dramatic discourse. We see the fine degree of difference between the two playwrights (amounting to a difference in kind) when we extract, say, the first ten directives in Act Two, starting with the end of the opening stage direction, and string them together with ellipses to indicate the omitted dialogue:

There is only one square stool left, on which Mallika sits, grinding medicinal herbs in a stone mortar. The corner of the bed in the inner room is visible as before. Ambika is lying on the bed. Every now and then, she turns on her side. Nikshep enters. Mallika adjusts her wrap. . . . Mallika sighs with resignation, and begins to pour the powdered medicine from the mortar into a bowl. Nikshep drags the second cane stool and sits down near her. . . . She adds milk and honey to the medicine and stirs it. Nikshep sits with his fingers intertwined, gazing at her. . . . Mallika averts her eyes and keeps stirring the medicine busily. . . . Mallika looks at him gravely. . . . Nikshep sighs deeply. . . . He gets up and starts pacing. . . . He pauses and looks at Mallika. . . . She stands up with the medicine. . . . She goes in and, helping Ambika to sit up, feeds her the medicine. Ambika swallows, then shakes her head. Nikshep strolls over to the lattice window. Outside, the sound of horses' hooves approaches, then recedes. Nikshep continues to watch from the window. Having taken her medicine, Ambika lies down. Mallika emerges from the inner room, and turns in the doorway to look

at Ambika. . . . Ambika nods. Mallika shuts the door.
Nikshep steps away from the window.

As such an exercise indicates immediately, Rakesh's direct
interventions in the stage directions seem to constitute a
continuous novelistic narrative—characterized as a *kathanak*
in his letter to Upendranath Ashk—that is fragmented and
distributed systematically inside the dramatic discourse as a
self-reflexive parallel.[19] Furthermore, given his compositional
practice as well as his theory of drama and theatre, Rakesh
views his work as an organic unity, or a whole with the
functional integrity of a machine, so his novelistic narrative
is thoroughly integrated in its conception with the text's
dramatic discourse.[20] As a consequence, the multifoliate stage
directions in *Ashadh* are addressed not only to 'readers of
the play', as in O'Neill, but also simultaneously to 'directors,
designers, and actors'—for all of whom the Hindi play-text
becomes a single, continuous medium for imagining 'a virtual
performance of the play that he has constructed as drama'.

Diegesis and Mimesis

The novelistic stage directions in *Ashadh* perform two vital
functions, directly on the page and in transfer to performance.
First, in refining his technique to this novel extreme, Rakesh
provocatively reverses the distribution of diegesis and mimesis
that is conventional in drama with classical-European origins.
In Plato and Aristotle, the diegetic mode of representation
consists of narration and narrative, description and exposition,
talking and 'telling', whereas the mimetic mode consists of
depiction and enactment, 'showing' and spectacle; Plato

valorizes diegesis, which produces the cerebral genre of the 'Socratic dialogue', but Aristotle advocates mimesis, which gives us the live theatre of tragedy and comedy and farce.[21] At a more complex level, modern plays—as well as films and television programmes—combine different measures of the mimetic and diegetic modes, but mostly subordinate the 'telling' in the performance (including the dialogue) to the 'showing' in a dynamic spectacle. Euro-American practice along Aristotelian lines therefore conceives of dramatic dialogue as primarily mimetic (an imitation of human speech that contributes squarely to the depiction of the action on the stage), and stage directions as essentially diegetic (descriptions, instructions, and guidelines in the author's voice), and hence to be left off the stage.

In contrast, the most important parts of the dialogue in *Ashadh* contain a great deal of diegetic material, and 'depict' the action obliquely, mainly through 'suggestion, resonance' and 'indirection, deviation' (*dhvani* and *vakrokti*, respectively, in both Hindi and Sanskrit); whereas the vivid, precisely visualized, and novelistic stage directions constitute the most mimetic components of the play—and hence, like Beckett's crypto-novelistic instructions in *Endgame* (1958), prove to be indispensable for its translation to the stage. This innovative, experimental dimension of *Ashadh* makes it a language-centred play to an exceptional extent, in a modernist style that echoes the historical Kalidas's own language-centred, predominantly diegetic plays. The unusual proportion and distribution of diegesis in the Hindi text explains why the performers at Anamika initially resisted it in Calcutta in 1960; but these features also highlight Rakesh's singular achievement in fusing the canons of classical Sanskrit drama with the conventions of mimesis to create a perfectly performable modernist play—a dozen years before Peter Brook launched his 'interculturalism' to pursue a 'neocolonialist' version of such a paradigm in England and France.[22]

The disposition of diegetic and mimetic elements in Rakesh's play-text can be pinpointed quite precisely. His stage directions consistently 'show' readers and performers what is or ought to be happening on the stage as he imagines it, thus transforming instruction into dramatic action itself and into its self-reflexive interpretation. Substantial stretches of dialogue (at the beginning of each act, for instance) are diegetic rather than mimetic because they 'tell' what has happened offstage without 'showing' it. Many of the turning points in the plot are only narrated, not depicted: among them, Mallika's experience of 'pure emotion' with Kalidas on the first day of the season of rain (Act One); Kalidas's transformation into Matrugupta and his life at the royal court (Act Two); Ambika's death and Mallika's actual degeneration into a life of prostitution and single-motherhood (between Acts Two and Three); Kalidas's composition of his famous mature works (between the end of Act One and the beginning of Act Three); and the final disintegration of his life of power and fame in Kashmir (just before Act Three). It is true that, in its basic orientation, all the dialogue is mimetic, but it is so only in the trivial sense of imitating conversation in real life; in the process of representing character, especially in the cases of Mallika, Ambika, Vilom, and Kalidas, what it does more forthrightly is to focus on the 'expression' of emotions, thoughts, attitudes, experiences, memories, and expectations mainly through the oblique suggestive power of words—and hence through diegesis. As an experienced fiction writer, Rakesh handles narration, description, and exposition so skilfully that we barely notice the minimization of mimesis, and the dialogue on the stage comes through as remarkably lively and lifelike, without foregrounding its discursive quality.

Genre and Classical Time-Space

The other function of Rakesh's novelistic stage directions is to delimit the genre of his play by intercepting its formal and modal features, and to complicate the setting of its dramatic action in the process. If *Ashadh* belonged to the class of historical drama, then its stage directions would not hesitate to identify the time and place of its action on the plane of 'material reality'. A well-defined history play such as Girish Karnad's *Tughlaq*, for instance, begins with an authorial direction—'A.D. 1327. The yard in front of the Chief Court of Justice in Delhi'—which establishes the historicity of the events to follow. If, however, a play incorporates characters, social practices, or other materials from a distant past, but does not intend to treat them historically, then the stage directions usually exclude specificity of time and place. The modernist theatrical conventions concerning these generic signifiers are clear, for instance, in Jean Anouilh's plays: his *Eurydice* (1941), where the two principal characters carry mythological names, dramatizes an ancient story *in* modern times (the 1930s), and hence starts with the explicit authorial notation that 'The action of the play takes place in the refreshment room of a French provincial railway station and in a hotel bedroom in Marseilles'; whereas his *Antigone* (first performed in French in 1944 and translated into English in 1946), which draws all its characters from Sophocles' ancient Greek work, seeks to develop parallels between the fictional action of his source and political events in mid-twentieth-century France, and hence does not specify the precise era to be represented in the mise en scène.

Although he may not have encountered Anouilh or *Antigone* in particular, Rakesh nevertheless aligns himself and experiments with the paradigm invoked in the French play. His stage directions and his list of dramatis personae mention only 'a village', without specifying either a historical date or a geographical location for the theatrical production: the only early clues to the era in which the action of *Ashadh* supposedly takes place are passing references in the dialogue, in the middle of Act One and at the beginning of Act Two. In the first of these instances, Matul asks rhetorically: 'Didn't I always tell you, Ambika, that the son of the son of the daughter of the founding father of our clan fought for the Gupta empire against the Shaka invaders?' But, given his characterization as a mostly unwitting buffoon, in the mould of the court jesters in the historical Kalidas's plays (such as Madhavya, the poor brahmin, in *The Recognition of Shakuntala*), Matul's chronological exactitude in this whimsical line is at best a parody, a tongue-in-cheek authorial swipe at historicity. Early in Act Two, when the more reliable Nikshep mentions the fictional Kalidas's marriage to 'a Gupta princess', the historical period of the action seems to be the turn of the fifth century, which is reinforced by the play's repeated references to Ujjayini as the 'imperial capital'—though this would have to mean the capital of the imperial *province* of Malwa (after

Chandragupta Vikramaditya's defeat of the Central Asian Shakas and consequent western expansion in the first decade of the new century), since the centre of empire itself remained at Pataliputra, some 800 km (500 miles) to the east.[23] The first half of the play thus deliberately leaves the date of its action in the penumbra of uncertainty, nested inside the folds of dialogue, and does not bring it into the light of the dramatist's discourse.

In comparison, Rakesh renders the geographical location of the mise en scène explicitly indeterminate. The list of dramatis personae as well as the stage directions—otherwise so meticulous—leave the village and its rural province unnamed. The dialogue steadily builds up a verbal picture of the surrounding landscape—but not the village itself—with fragments in Mallika's references to mountains, valleys, clouds, rain, and birds in Act One, followed by more picturesque details during the royal party's visit in Act Two. But if, at the end, we assemble all of the text's information about topography, geological features, flora and fauna (specimens of which Priyangumanjari wants to carry to Kashmir), weather and climate, animal husbandry (Matul's herds and Vilom's bees), agricultural products (the grain that Ambika winnows), and so on, we are forced to reach the conclusion that there is no one physical location anywhere in India—as we know it today—where all those elements actually exist together, the way they do in the play. Just as the historical Kalidas's works, such as *A Gathering of Seasons* and *The Recognition of Shakuntala*, famously combine elements drawn from all over the subcontinent into a single imaginary locus to achieve representativeness, Rakesh appears to set *Ashadh* in a speculative time and a hypothetical place that do not have unambiguous correlates in historical, geographical, and environmental fact. The portrait of 'classical India' that *Ashadh* offers thus is a fictive, dramatic construction that serves aesthetic functions in the time and space of 'literature' rather than 'history'—and is literary rather than literal.

Rakesh builds this world on three distinct planes, on each of which, in M.M. Bakhtin's words, 'Time, as it were, thickens, takes on flesh, becomes artistically visible', and 'likewise, space becomes charged and responsive to the movements of time, plot and history', but *outside* the circles of empirical history and geography.[24] At one level, the novelistic stage directions play a decisive role in the picture-making: on the page, they propel the reader's 'willing suspension of disbelief', and his or her active participation in the construction of the drama and its meanings; and, in the theatre, they drive the entire company's construction of the mise en scène itself, both materially and metaphorically. At another level, the dialogue is just as constitutive of the play's vivid representation: both the choice and the order of words—'Sanskritized' Hindi in the original and a mostly 'middle' Anglo-Saxon diction in our translation, housed inside the syntax and rhythm of modulated prose—are as vital to the production of moving images of a supposedly classical world in the mind's eye as on the physical stage. And, through and behind and before these, the dynamics of characterization fleshes out the plot at a third level, amalgamating the self-presentation and self-understanding of the characters, their decorum in monologue and dialogue, their individual conduct and mutual interactions, and their measured balance between classical 'public exteriority' and modernist 'interiority'.[25] But all three planes coincide with each other in the time-space of *Ashadh*, to constitute the self-consistent and self-sufficient dramatic action that we take to be its image of classical India.

The net effect of Rakesh's authorial interventions in the play is to position his postcolonial modernist classicism as the antithesis of the anti-modern classicism of a writer such as T.S. Eliot, simultaneously classicizing the modern and modernizing the classical, but outside the circumference of Europe. Rakesh's past is never merely the past, just as his present is never merely the present, and the presence of the past is matched by the reciprocal pastness of the present, with past and present coexisting in 'the time of literature', which is not merely 'the time of history'. This aesthetic time is not the time in which 'the whole of the literature of Europe from Homer and within it the whole of the literature of his own country has a simultaneous existence and composes a simultaneous order'—rather, it is the 'house of being' *inside the Indian languages*, in which the habilitation of Sanskrit within the interstices of Hindi repairs some of the havoc of 'unhousedness' that European colonialism left behind, on the soil of India's 'indigenous' traditions, after more than two hundred years of economic and cultural depredation.[26]

Rakesh's overwhelming existential drive seems to have been to set this house in order, to engender the personal and collective self-transformation necessary for a postcolonial reorientation to it, beginning inside domestic space—as in his final finished play, *Adhe adhure* (Half Formed, Half Unfinished, 1969)—but extending all the way into the social and public spheres. For him, the objective as well as the means of such a metamorphosis was to incorporate the classical Sanskrit ideal of *auchitya* (aptness, appropriateness, fitness, propriety, congruity) into Indian modernity, much as Joyce's Stephen Daedalus incorporates Aquinas's formula for pulchritude ('wholeness, harmony and resonance') into Anglo-Irish modernism.[27] *Ashadh*, in this context, is a master work of *auchitya*, aimed against the existential and postcolonial 'disorder of things' sprawling all around it—not as a principle of 'moral propriety' or 'formalist decorum', as it is often restrictively construed, but rather as a living principle of *aesthetic order* which, as both Abhinavagupta at the end of the tenth century and Wallace Stevens in the mid-twentieth understood, is the principle of 'order' itself.

Appendices

These Appendices provide translations from six sources in which Mohan Rakesh comments on *Ashadh ka ek din*, before, during, and after its composition. The material is arranged chronologically by genre, and spans the period from 1958 to 1968. All the translations are as literal as possible, but also aim to convey the flavour of Rakesh's styles of personal and critical prose (in diary entries, correspondence, and published commentary). Editorial notes and insertions in the appendices are enclosed in brackets, including some citations, page numbers, and ellipses that indicate omissions or discontinuities in the translations. Ellipses without brackets are Rakesh's own. The Hindi sources are cited in either the headnotes or the endnotes; they are listed in full bibliographic form under Rakesh in the Works Cited at the end of this volume. Appendices 2, 3, 5, and 6 are all translated from Nemichandra Jain, ed., *Mohan rakesh ke sampurna natak* (The Complete Plays of Mohan Rakesh, 1993); for brevity, this source is cited in the endnotes as *CP*.

1. Select Entries from Rakesh's Diary, 1958–59

[Translated from *Mohan rakesh ki dayari* (The Diary of Mohan Rakesh, 1985). The page numbers provided for the following entries refer to this edition. Our selection seeks to cover all the passages in the diary that refer to *Ashadh ka ek din*. Rakesh's first language here is Hindi, written in the Devanagari script; but he intersperses it with words, phrases, sentences, and whole entries in English, written either in the roman or the Devanagari script. In this appendix, we have reserved italics for expressions that appear in English in the original (in either script). We have preserved the English acronym *AKED* wherever Rakesh uses it for the play.]

JALANDHAR, 9 FEBRUARY 1958 [P. 163]
I have decided to write a full length drama on Kalidas, before starting on the novel.

Shall set about it tomorrow.
Should complete it by the 21st.

JALANDHAR, 13 FEBRUARY 1958 [P. 163]
[At this time Rakesh was planning to leave for Delhi latest by 1 March.]
I shall try to write out the play on Kalidas during the days that I am here.

JALANDHAR, 18 APRIL 1958 [P. 165]
Even though I finished the play, it didn't get finished—I still can't get hold of the last part.

JALANDHAR, 2 MAY 1958 [P. 166]

Started writing *full-length play* 'Ashadh ka ek din' on 3 March, finished it on 21 April. That's how things are with me.

JALANDHAR, 1 SEPTEMBER 1958 [P. 201]

I received Namvar [Singh]'s review of 'Ashadh ka ek din'. . . .

It seems that the play is really well written. Otherwise I cannot understand why everybody should praise it.

I wrote short stories for ten years—no one ever showered them with such free-throated praise. [Upendranath] Ashk, Jagdishchandra Mathur, Lakshmichandra Jain, Chaman [Lal]— I've received the same sort of praise in all their letters—and I'd thought that given the historical touch [in the play] most of my friends would make faces and say, 'Wow, kiddo, trying to feed off History's belly now, are we? That lifelong capital you'd accumulated—did you eat it all up?'

JALANDHAR, 10 SEPTEMBER 1958 [P. 206]

A letter arrived from Rajpal and Sons today saying that the first edition of 'Ashadh ka ek din' is sold out. This news really made me very happy. But along with the joy, there's also a doubt. I don't know how many copies there were in the first edition. Two thousand or one thousand? But these days no one publishes an edition of less than 2000 copies. And if it was an edition of 2000, then how did it sell out in just two and a half or three months?

JALANDHAR, 20 SEPTEMBER 1958 [P. 209]

I felt utterly dejected when I learnt from Rajpal and Sons' letter that they'd published a first edition of 'Ashadh ka ek din' of just 1000 copies.

JALANDHAR, 5 NOVEMBER 1958 [P. 216]

Ramesh [Pal] has written to say that Rangmanch has received a grant of Rs 300 from the [Uttar Pradesh state] government for a performance of 'Ashadh ka ek din', and they'll get other facilities as well. They may present the play in mid-December. I was delighted with the news . . . but will I myself be able to go see the *performance*?

NEW DELHI, 6 FEBRUARY 1959 [PP. 226–27]

Spent the first two days with Ramesh Pal. Came to know that 'Ashadh ka ek din' was first performed in Nagpur on the occasion of the convention of the Congress party (*not yet confirmed*), and then it was performed by Rangmanch in Lucknow on the 10th [of January, 1959]. Sarvadanand Verma, Bhagavati Charan Verma, Amritlal Nagar, etcetera, remained *antagonistic*. Then it was performed on the 21st during the Theatre Festival, where it won the Best Production *award*. It also got several other *prizes*. The papers that they sent never reached me. Ramesh had asked me to come especially for the *performance* of the 21st. If he'd mentioned the reason for the invitation in his telegram, then I'd definitely have attended, but . . .

Now the playwrights here are trying to *run down* the play on the grounds that, in Lucknow, Babu Sampurnanand refused to inaugurate the performance because he'd been told that it demeans Kalidas. *What people* . . . I've already accepted that the Sangeet Natak Akademi *prize* will go to somebody else— even though [Suresh] Awasthi said the other day, 'Brother, the *rumour* is that it will win the prize. *It is very high up.*' I don't know. Nor do I want to know. One's sleep is ruined pointlessly. . . . I feel exasperated only on account of my publishers—

otherwise, except for living on the *royalties* of my books, I don't want to entertain hopes or expectations of anything else. But how to make it possible? How? One publisher has sent Rs 24 as payment for a six-month account period, and another has sent Rs 8 as the balance for a year! *Heavens!*

NEW DELHI, 23 AUGUST 1959 [PP. 227–28]
. . . On the night of the 9th there was news on the radio that the Sangeet Natak Akademi's [annual] award for the best Hindi play [of 1958] has been given to 'Ashadh ka ek din'. From that moment to now—I just don't know how these two weeks have flown by so quickly. Parties, functions, articles, criticism, bursts of laughter, and, in the midst of it all, a profound, unfathomable sadness—why this sadness has beset me, I can't say. Can't say what process the prize has begun in my subconscious to produce this effect.

NEW DELHI, 29 SEPTEMBER 1959 [P. 228]
I was obsessed with the idea that we'd *produce* the play ourselves—that was the one thought taking hold of my heart and mind. Gave it up finally—writing is the foremost thing, nothing else is.

NEW DELHI, 23 OCTOBER 1959 [P. 228]
Last night they broadcast AKED as a national play. I felt like committing suicide after listening to it. And I feel like destroying all that I have written of the novel.

NEW DELHI, 12 DECEMBER 1959 [P. 229]
First steps were taken today in connection with the production of AKED.

2. Preface to the First Edition of *Ashadh ka ek din* (June 1958)

Drama in Hindi has no links with any particular theatrical tradition. All we have before us are the accomplishments of Western theatre. But the conditions of our life do not ask for those accomplishments, nor does it seem possible for us to consecrate that theatrecraft amongst us on a large scale without any changes.

The idea of the development of the Hindi stage certainly does not imply that government or semi-governmental institutions should come up with performance spaces equipped with ultramodern facilities here and there so that Hindi plays may be presented in them. The question is not merely one of financial convenience but also of a certain cultural vision. The Hindi stage will have to take a leading role in representing the cultural achievements and aspirations of the Hindi-speaking region, in expressing the richness and variety of our aesthetic sensibilities. The kind of stage that is needed to present the colourful texture of our daily life, to express our sensations and pulsations, will be quite different from the Western stage. The constitutive features of this stage will come to life with the help of theatrical experimentation, and it will continue its development in the hands of capable actors and directors.

It is possible that this play may contribute something towards the search for those possibilities.[1]

3. Preface to the Second Edition of *Ashadh ka ek din* (September 1958)

I am happy that the second edition of this play is going to press just three months after its original publication. I am grateful to the friends who have sent me their expressions of support regarding the play. Some friends in Lucknow and Delhi had even made plans to present the play on stage, but those have not been put into practice as yet. I believe that the real value of a dramatic work—its success or failure—is decided only on the stage. If good, successful plays are to be written, it really would be appropriate to expect that they be performed on stage before publication, and be given their final textual form only in light of that experience. But I think it will take us some years to get to such a phase. All three acts in this play have the same set, so I think that staging it will require very few resources. However, the main roles—especially those of Kalidas, Mallika, and Vilom—will require very skilful actors. With this edition, I also wanted to provide descriptions of costumes, etc., for all the characters, but I am unable to do so for lack of time. I hope that in the next edition I will be able to provide all those descriptions. Some people are under a misconception about the last act of the play. They have come to the conclusion that, by this time in the action, the relationship between Mallika and Vilom is one of husband and wife. This actually is not the case. At this point, Mallika is not Vilom's wife but a woman who lives by the commerce of her body because of her destitute condition—and this circumstance becomes clear through the dialogue and other indications in the plot.

The play contains some symbolic gestures towards life in our own times—chief among them is the issue of the poet's acceptance of state patronage. Critics have different views about whether or not these gestures help to strengthen the effect of the play's core emotions. My own opinion is that, without these indicators, it would not have been possible to properly express the core emotions of the play and the painful irony of the life of Kalidas and Mallika.

Aside from one or two words, I have not made any changes in the play.[2]

4. Excerpt from a Letter to Upendranath Ashk, 1958

[Rakesh's letter to friend and fellow writer Upendranath Ashk is dated 7 August 1958. He wrote it in Hindi, but interspersed it occasionally with English expressions, which are preserved in italics. Within the quotations from the play, the italics come from our translation. The page numbers that Rakesh provides for his quotations are different from those of our translation; we have inserted the latter in brackets after his.]

[. . .] I was very happy to read your response to the play (although I feel *guilty* that I still haven't managed to send copies to you and Pathakji). My local circle of friends here carried off the copies that I'd received, and I've been writing to Rajpal & Sons for several days, but the additional copies haven't arrived as yet. I've written the play strictly for the stage, so I'd also like to know your thoughts about its actability.

So far as the third act is concerned, I believe you've misconstrued it a bit. Mallika isn't Vilom's wife by marriage, and Vilom isn't the only man who has taken advantage of her destitution. This circumstance should have been made clear by the following indications. Pages 100–101 [see p. 170]—'No one else could be the fullness, the feeling, that you were in me, but this womb of emptiness contains so many, many images of someone else! Do you know—I've lost my name and acquired an adjective in its place, and now, in my own eyes, I'm not a name but just an adjective.'

'The traders had said there is gossip in Ujjayini—that you spend a lot of your time in the company of courtesans. . . . But have you seen *this* face of a courtesan? Can you recognize me today?'

Pages 115–116 [see pp. 182–83]—'Vilom's no longer an uninvited guest in this home. Now he enters it by right.' [. . .]

'That's why I was about to say, it's possible that Kalidas may be able to look and tell [if . . .] the little girl's features really resemble Vilom's features, or . . . ?'

In my view, this play is really the *tragedy* of Mallika—not of Kalidas or Vilom. She encourages Kalidas and sends him to Ujjayini, but with that she creates *emotional chaos* for herself. Then, when Kalidas doesn't come to meet her while he's on his way to Kashmir, and the gift meant for him just lies around, her *tragedy is accentuated*. And when Kalidas returns at the end, after having his own say and making his own inferences about her circumstances, he merely leaves again. Kalidas undoubtedly leaves with the *impression* that Mallika is leading a married life with Vilom. Before he arrives, what Mallika says about herself is addressed only to the blank book. After Kalidas's arrival, there's no stage direction for Mallika that could make her situation clear to him, but there are a lot of small hints to the viewer, because the viewer has already begun to know her in the guise of a prostitute. The fact that Vilom knocks on the door, and then goes away after saying, 'The door's always shut . . . *hunh* . . . the door's always shut!' [see p. 173] also illuminates the actual situation for the viewer, even though it doesn't for Kalidas. In this perspective, the end of the play takes Mallika's tragedy to a *climax*, where she hears what he has to say, but isn't able to say anything of her own to him, isn't able to explain her present condition. And her daughter is what's holding her tight—and, because of her, she's unable to cross the threshold of her home. Vilom's *tragedy* is that he knows he has taken advantage of Mallika's destitution and possessed her body, but hasn't been able to get her feelings for Kalidas out of her mind. He's a defeated man even in his victory. And the *irony* of the whole play is that, even when Kalidas came back, he went away again harbouring only a misconception—Mallika's years of anguish still couldn't find expression.

Don't know whether or not I managed this the way I wanted to. In this regard, please read the third act again and write back to me at length. [. . .][3]

5. Preface to the First Edition of *Laharon ke rajhans* (1963)

After *Ashadh ka ek din*, this is my second play.

Many kinds of arguments arose in relation to the first play, regarding its historical accuracy, its theatrical possibilities, and, most of all, its portrayal of the character of Kalidas. The doubts about its theatrical possibilities really have been answered to a great extent already. The play has been performed successfully in Delhi, Calcutta, Lucknow, Allahabad, Nagpur, Kanpur, Gwalior, and a number of other places. A director like [Ebrahim] Alkazi and an organization like Anamika have taken it up and presented it from entirely different points of view. It has also been broadcast in all the Indian languages from various regional centres of All India Radio.

The objections to the characterization of Kalidas merely express some people's ingrained prejudices. There is a class of researchers that has treated Kalidas and Matrugupta as the same individual historically. This is exactly the basis on which Jai Shankar Prasad has imagined Kalidas's character in *Skanda-gupta*. Then there is another class of researchers that does not accept the validity of such an interpretation—but how many indisputable facts about Kalidas's life have been available to us so far? All the materials we have are based on some conjecture or other. It is a different matter, of course, that some people find their own conjectures to be more valid than those of others.

One critic wrote that 'In the play, a disciplined, ascetic, great soul like Kalidas has been pictured as a weak man'. I was surprised because the critic in question is a good Sanskrit scholar. If this is the character of Kalidas that has emerged in his mind after reading *The Recognition of Shakuntala*, *The Origin of the Young God*, and *The Cloud-Messenger*, then what can be said? When traditionalist attitudes and beliefs take over a person's intelligence, it is pointless to expect anything else. Our tradition is such that we always want to place our civilizational symbols on a superhuman plane. Any evidence of ordinary humanity in them hurts us. The principal reason for this may be that we have no trust in our own humanity, no faith in our own reality. Since we expect nothing from ourselves, it seems impossible to us that one can remain on a human level and still accomplish something great. That greatness is possible *only* at a human level—this would be too hard for us even to contemplate.

Whatever the character of Kalidas is in *Ashadh ka ek din*, it is not very far removed from the personality implicit in his works; but, yes, it has been altered a little for the purpose of making it viable as a modern symbol. This is so because, for me, Kalidas is not a person but a symbol of our creative energies and, in the play, this symbol is meant to signify the inner conflict that drives the artistic imagination in any historical age. Whether the person called Kalidas had to pass through such an inner conflict or not—that is an insignificant issue. The main point is that, in every era, many have had to pass through it, and we ourselves are among those who are passing through it now. It is even possible that 'Kalidas' may not be the real name of this person, but I could not find a better label, a better signifier, for our cumulative creative energies up to this point in time.

The Kalidas of *Ashadh ka ek din* is not weak; he is vulnerable, unstable, and harrowed by his inner struggles. Vilom, who appears to be strong in comparison, points to the destructive forces of abnegation. This man has devoured the struggle within him, and hence is relatively more composed. The voice of despair and scepticism is manifestly more powerful than that of hope and faith—this is just what it expects from itself in order to establish itself. The forces of hope and faith may seem to be weak in their vulnerability, but it is worth stating that they do not suffer defeat at the hands of barbaric forces. In *Ashadh ka ek din*, the defeated man is not the despairing Kalidas, but the self-possessed Vilom, because these two characters are not in themselves the signifiers of victory and defeat—that signifier is Mallika, who is the fully articulated form of Kalidas's faith. Mallika's character is not only that of lover and muse, but also of that rooted, unwavering constancy which is not destroyed at its source even though it withers on the surface.

Dependence on history or historical figures does not turn literature into history. History accumulates facts, and presents them in a temporal sequence. This has never been the objective of literature. Filling the empty chambers of history is also not an area of accomplishment for literature. Literature is not bound by the time of history, it articulates history inside time; it does not separate one era from another, but joins many eras together. In this way, the 'today' and 'tomorrow' of history do not remain the 'today' and 'tomorrow' of literature; instead, they become some moments joined together in the boundlessness of time in a way which makes them indivisible from the viewpoint of signalling a direction in life. For this reason, history is not expressed in literature through its incontrovertible events, but through an imagination that links events together and creates a distinct, new history of its own kind. This creation is not history in the conventional sense. To look for that kind of history one really should go to the scholarly tomes of historians.

The foundation of the play presented here [*Laharon ke rajhans* (The Royal Swans of the Waves)] is also historical, but only in the sense of the term denoted by this explication.

The basis of the story is Ashvaghosha's poem *Saundarananda*
[Handsome Nand] but because of the reconfiguration of
circumstances in the fullness of time, it is also imaginary.
Ashvaghosha's *Saundarananda* is imagined as well, because
he reconfigured the story available in Sanskrit and Pali
literature from his own point of view, and elaborated it with
an imagined unity of time, place, and action. In influence and
magnitude, the story of *Saundarananda* goes much further
than the story of Nand and Sundari in the commentary on
the *Dhammapada*. The facts about the lives of Nand and
Sundari in *Saundarananda* are quite different from the limited
historical facts available about their lives, and the kinds of
accurate facts that are found in scholarly tomes are in fact
not available in their cases at all. Even the stories about them
in Sanskrit and Pali sources differ greatly. If an author today
exercises the same freedom in going beyond the facts of
Saundarananda that the author of *Saundarananda* exercised
in relation to the facts available to him, the people deeply
devoted to ancient texts should not be taken aback. They can
find the satisfaction of history based on facts in a different
place, and should not search for it in this play. The story of
Nand and Sundari here is merely a launching pad, because I
felt that it could be reconfigured in time. The fundamental
inner conflict in this play is modern in the same sense in
which its equivalent is modern in *Ashadh ka ek din*. How the
play will unfold upon the stage is impossible to predict at
this time. Like *Ashadh ka ek din*, this play, too, could not be
tested on the stage before its publication in print. I would
like to hope that, like the earlier venture, this one, too, will
make a place for itself.[4]

6. Excerpt from the Preface to the Third Edition of *Laharon ke rajhans* (1968)

[Rakesh's preface to the third edition of *Laharon ke rajhans* (The Royal Swans of the Waves) is exceptionally long and multifarious. The following translation excerpts only two paragraphs from it, which offer unique and important comments on the composition of *Ashadh ka ek din* and on Rakesh's method of composition. The paragraphs come from different parts of the preface, and hence are separated by ellipses in square brackets and a line space.]

The version in which this play [*Laharon ke rajhans*] was published in 1963 had been started before I wrote *Ashadh ka ek din*. By then I had gained control over a mental obstacle. I was beginning to see more clearly in my mind how a historical context could be used in relation to one's present—especially for these two plot lines which had been in my mind for a long time in the shape of the two [Sanskrit] lines, 'On the first day of *ashadh* . . .' and 'The royal swans upon the waves'. *Ashadh ka ek din* was written during the months of March and April in 1958. I did not complete *Laharon ke rajhans* first because I was dissatisfied with every earlier effort to do so, and felt that it would be better to write another play first instead of getting absorbed yet again in this one. Three characters in *Ashadh ka ek din* were also already clear in my mind. While reading *The Cloud-Messenger*, I used to feel that its story is not so much about the banished *yaksha* as it is about the poet exiled from his own soul, who had poured his feelings of guilt into this work of the imagination. The three characters that

I discovered while thinking about these feelings of guilt were those of Mallika, Ambika, and Vilom. Kalidas's character was, of course, already at the centre. Apart from these, the rest are filler characters whom I created while writing the play. *Ashadh ka ek din* was published in June 1958. The reactions to it that I received immediately upon publication gave me, on the one hand, the self-confidence to write other plays; but, on the other hand, they also filled my mind with frustration towards this play [*Laharon ke rajhans*] that I had begun earlier. For two years I kept wanting to finish it, but also kept postponing it from one day to the next. [. . .]

After that, in 1960 and 1961, this play [*Laharon ke rajhans*] was written twice, without being completed on either occasion. The first time at Raison (Kullu) and the second time at Gulmarg. Both times, I could not finish it because of the pressure of personal circumstances. It is a personal difficulty with me that if I leave any work unfinished, I am unable to pick up the writing later and move it forward from that point—if the interval is longer than, say, three to four days, then the next time I have to begin all over again, from a fresh starting point. This has happened with many other works, and it has been happening especially with this play. If early in 1962 I had not taken up the editorship of *Sarika*, then I would have tried once more to finish it. But that whole year passed in dealing with the job, and I picked up this play again in the month of April 1963—a few days after I had left the position.[5]

Notes

These notes are divided into two sections: General Notes and Explanatory and Dramaturgical Notes to the Play. The *General Notes* cover four broad topics: the transcription and spelling of terms and expressions from languages other than English, whether Indian or European; the pronunciation of characters' names in the play; significant twentieth-century Indian writers other than Rakesh who are mentioned or discussed in this book; and the progressive and modernist literary movements in postcolonial Hindi, which serve as contexts for Rakesh's work. The *Explanatory and Dramaturgical Notes to the Play* focus on the text. They gloss specific names, terms, objects, and meanings that may be familiar to different degrees to various groups of readers in India and outside; but they also provide information and interpretations that may assist directors, actors, designers, and technical stage personnel in conceptualizing a production.

GENERAL NOTES

Transcription and Spelling

Terms from eighteen Indian and non-Indian languages appear in roman transcription in this book. If a term of foreign origin has been naturalized in English, we have followed *The Oxford Dictionary of English*, 3rd ed. (2010) for its orthography, spelling, grammatical forms, etc. (hence, mise en scène is in roman type). For unassimilated Greek, Latin, French, and German terms, we have followed standard practices in international scholarly discourse; wherever choices needed to be made, we have opted for forms that we prefer (e.g., *muthos* rather than *mythos* in the case of Greek). We translate all those terms from the European languages that may be unfamiliar to general readers, or may have technical meanings, when we use them for the first time (e.g., *mise en abyme*); and provide further explanations in our commentary, as needed.

We follow the same pattern for terms and expressions in Sanskrit, Hindi, and other Indian languages; hence our use of the *ODE*'s forms for such words as acharya—with brahman, kshatriya, vaishya, and shudra adapted to the same orthographic style (no italics or initial capitals). For Indian-language terms that have not been absorbed into English, we use italics at every occurrence, and provide a translation on the first occasion, using quotation marks or parentheses (e.g., *kathanak* and *pratik*, mentioned early in the Afterword). After much debate, we have chosen *not* to use diacritical marks for accurate transcription; instead, we have approximated the standard spelling and pronunciation in the Devanagari script system with roman transcriptions.

Our system here is designed for general readers worldwide, and is a compact and simplified version of a technical linguistic system. In our transcriptions: *a* is used for both the short vowel ('*a*bout' or 'b*u*t') and the long ('f*a*ther'); likewise, *i* is used for the short ('s*i*t') and the long ('f*ee*t'); *u* also is used for the short ('p*u*t') and the long ('c*oo*l'); whereas *o* represents only one sound ('h*o*pe'). For the diphthongs: *e* stands for the sound in 'm*a*ke'; *ai* is a glide from *a* to *i*, in which the latter two vowels may be either short (as in Hindi k*ai*se, how) or long (as in Hindi *bh*ai, brother); and *au* is a glide from short *a* to short *u* (as in Hindi k*au*n, who). Exceptions to these rules include words such as *nai* (feminine 'new'), where the *a* is short and the *i* is long, so that an alternative transcription would be *nayi* (parallel to the masculine, *naya*). Among consonants, the main divergence from English is in the letter *n*, which represents four of the five Indian nasals—velar ('thi*ng*'), palatal ('pi*n*ch'), retroflex (stronger than 'ti*n*t'), and dental ('si*n*')—as well as the nasalization of all vowels and diphthongs (e.g., in Hindi plural endings, as in *kahaniyan*, stories). Moreover, both Indian sibilants (palatal and retroflex) are simplified to *sh* (English palatal '*sh*ock').

For Sanskrit terms (including Vedic forms), we have spelt out all the vowels; in the case of long nominal compounds that may be hard to decipher in English, we have used hyphens to indicate convenient 'breaks'; hence *Meghaduta*, *Kumara-sambhava*, and *Abhijnana-shakuntala*. With great reluctance, we have left out distinctions between short and long vowels, and have used the same transcription for both; hence, *Meghaduta*, rather than *Meghadoota*, even though the latter is closer to the correct articulation in speech.

For Hindi, we have followed the widespread modern practice of transcribing words as they are pronounced rather than as they are written, except for vowels (as above), or when a seemingly logical English transcription may be seriously misleading. Hence, we render the Hindi title of the play itself as *Ashadh ka ek din*, rather than as *Aashaadha kaa eka dina*; and we write *chhaya* (shadow), in order to distinguish the aspirated *chh* from the unaspirated *ch* in the absence of diacritical marks. In general, readers in the wider Anglophone world should be able to work with our transcriptions of Hindi expressions the way they do with transcriptions of Indian words in the international press (newspapers, magazines, websites). We have transcribed place names and modern Indian personal names the way they are most often romanized (in journalism and telephone directories, and on the Internet). We have named places and spelt their names the way they were named and spelt in Rakesh's adult lifetime (from the 1940s to the 1970s); hence, Bombay and Calcutta, and not Mumbai and Kolkata. In cases with multiple spellings, such as Jalandhar and Kullu, we have chosen present-day official spellings. With many Indian personal names, we have used the forms that the individuals themselves have fixed in English or that have become commonplace (e.g., Mohan Rakesh, Girish Karnad, Rabindranath Tagore, Agyeya, Kamleshwar); with names or forms that are not common in English, we have broadly followed the practice of romanization in Indian journalism and public discourse (e.g., Sarvadanand Verma).

The names of the dramatis personae in *Ashadh* pose special problems. As the Explanatory and Dramaturgical Notes to the Play below explain, Rakesh derives all his characters' names from Sanskrit; and by our own rules for transcription, we ought to spell them like the other Sanskrit terms here. But these Sanskritized names occur in a Hindi play, and hence are pronounced on stage as though they were assimilated into the language. We therefore have spelt and romanized the characters' names as though they were 'Hindi' names: hence, Dantul and Nikshep, not Dantula and Nikshepa. Our choice of 'Kalidas' for the play's fictional protagonist is consistent with this pattern; but, in the Introduction and Afterword and elsewhere, we discuss him in relation to 'the historical Kalidas' whose name, by our rules, ought to be transcribed as 'Kalidasa'. To avoid confusion of all sorts, we have finally chosen to spell and transcribe the name of both the fictive protagonist *and* the classical poet as 'Kalidas' uniformly throughout this book.

Pronunciation of the Characters' Names

In silent reading as in public performance, it is essential to pronounce the characters' names as accurately as possible in relation to their Hindi forms and Sanskrit origins. Except for the following nine vowels and consonants, all the letters in the characters' romanized names should be pronounced as in standard international English. The exceptions are:

a	like *u* in 'but'
a	like *a* in 'father'
i	like *i* in 'bit'
i	like *ee* in 'feet'
u	like *u* in 'put'
A	like *a* in 'gate'

o   like *o* in 'rote'
t   like the first *t* in French *tout*
d   like *th* in 'bathe' or 'father'

If we follow the above code, separate the syllables in each transcribed name using hyphens, and use s to indicate a stressed syllable and u to indicate an unstressed one, then we can approximate the Hindi pronunciation and stress-pattern in each case as follows:

Ambika	*am*-bi-**ka**	SUS
Mallika	m*al*-li-**ka**	SUS
Kalidas	ka-li-*d*as	SUS
Dantul	*d*an-*tu*l	SU
Matul	ma-*tu*l	SU
Nikshep	nik-sh*A*p	US
Vilom	wi-lom	US
Rangini	r*ang*-i-**ni**	SUS
Sangini	s*ang*-i-**ni**	SUS
Anusvar	*a*-n*u*-sw*a*r	UUS
Anunasik	*a*-n*u*-na-s*i*k	UUSU
Priyangumanjari	pri-*yang*-*u* / m*a*n-ja-**ri**	USU / SUS

The last two names on this list may pose some difficulty, which can be resolved by articulating each syllable fully and clearly, and—in the final case—by 'splitting' the long name in the middle with a slight pause (indicated by the forward slash in the last two columns).

References to Other Writers

The commentary and other material in this book refer to several Hindi writers who play significant roles in Mohan Rakesh's life, career, or writing in different ways and to different degrees; our critical discussion also assumes some familiarity with late-colonial and early-postcolonial literary movements in Hindi. Both these may be annotated as follows.

Predecessors and Older Contemporaries

JAI SHANKAR PRASAD (1889–1937) was a prominent figure in the Hindi literary movement known as *chhayavad* ('shadow-ism') in the 1920s and 1930s, along with Suryakant Tripathi (Nirala), Mahadevi Verma, and Sumitranandan Pant; the movement was named derisively by a critic after the title of one of Prasad's works. An aesthete and a high classicist best known for his lyric and epic poetry, he developed a near-obscurantist style of Sanskritized Hindi in verse and prose. He also experimented with anti-theatrical literary drama and the history play; *Skandagupta*, for instance, deals with an emperor of the Gupta dynasty and with Kalidas in the classical period, and is one of Rakesh's key reference points for *Ashadh*, in its conception and writing as well as its subsequent critical discussion.[1]

UPENDRANATH ASHK (1910–1996) was born in Jalandhar and spent a few years each in Lahore, Amritsar, Delhi, and Bombay, before settling for life in Allahabad in 1948. Beside some poetry, he published volumes of short stories, novels, and plays. A Punjabi Saraswat Brahmin, he started his writing career in Urdu; Premchand urged him to switch to Hindi, and wrote a foreword to his second collection of stories in 1933; Ashk followed the advice, but struggled for a while, composing everything in Urdu before rendering it in Hindi. He became a premier representative of 'progressive realism' in the latter language in the late 1930s. As a young man, Ashk worked as a journalist for Lala Lajpat Rai's nationalist newspaper and other anti-colonial publications; in the 1940s, he worked at All India Radio, Delhi, and at Filmistan, the major cinema studio in Bombay, where he established long-term connections with other writers employed with him or working in these cities, such as Saadat Hasan Manto, Khwaja Ahmed Abbas, Krishan Chander, and Rajinder Singh Bedi in Urdu, and S.H. Vatsyayan (Agyeya), Jainendra Kumar, and Girija Kumar Mathur in Hindi.

Rakesh and Ashk shared strong ties to Jalandhar; a common linguistic, socioeconomic, and cultural background (though they belonged to different caste groups); comparable literary interests; and personal connections to the other five cities mentioned above. Between the mid-1950s and the early 1970s, Ashk and his third wife, Kaushalya, carried on an extensive three-way correspondence with Rakesh—for whom they served as close friends, advisers, and surrogate 'elders'. Rakesh and the Ashks visited each other (in Allahabad and Delhi, respectively), stayed in each other's homes, travelled together, and networked for each other in literary circles. The Ashks provided much-needed emotional and practical support during the disintegration of Rakesh's first two marriages, his legal battle over visitation rights to his eldest son, and his unconventional wedding with his third wife, Anita Aulak. Ashk's wide-ranging social and literary contacts as well as his literary opinions—though politically to the left of Rakesh's modernism—had a direct impact on the latter's thinking, writing, and career.[2]

The Nai Kahani *Group*

The *nai kahani*, or 'new story', took off in Hindi by the mid-1950s as the work of a group or coterie, rather than as an organized literary movement. The writers identified most with it are Mohan Rakesh, Rajendra Yadav, Mannu Bhandari, Kamleshwar, Nirmal Verma, and Bhisham Sahni. Among them, Rakesh was the eldest by a few years, and he, Yadav, Bhandari, and Kamleshwar constituted the coterie from which much of the movement's energy flowed. Rakesh was closer in age to this group than to Ashk; while his relationship with the Ashk couple was always tempered by respect and relative formality, his friendships with the three younger people—who were regular correspondents when not in the same city—were intimate.

RAJENDRA YADAV (1929–2013), one of Rakesh's closest lifelong friends, was a key figure in the 'new story' and 'new novel' (*naya upanyas*) movements in Hindi. He was born in Agra and educated at Agra University (graduated 1951), but settled in Delhi in the 1960s. In 1986, he relaunched *Hans*, the premier literary magazine in Hindi started by Premchand in 1930, which had ceased publication in 1953; over the next twenty-seven years, he edited more than 300 monthly issues without a break, changing the complexion and tone of contemporary Hindi literary and public discourse (see also Kamleshwar below).

MANNU BHANDARI (b. 1931), educated at Calcutta University (1949) and Banaras Hindu University (1951), was the principal woman writer in both movements in Hindi fiction. Married to Rajendra Yadav for over four decades, she co-wrote the novel *Ek inch muskan* (The One-Inch Smile) with him in 1975, a unique experiment in Hindi by two major writers. Yadav's first novel, *Sara akash* (The Whole Sky, 1951; this Hindi title was given to it in the 1960s), was the basis of Basu Chatterjee's film of the same name (1969), an inaugural work in India's parallel or 'middle' cinema movement (positioned between commercial cinema and art-house film). Bhandari's famous story, *'Yahi sach hai'* ('This Is What Is True'), became the basis for Chatterjee's *Rajanigandha* (Night-Fragrance, 1974; Best Film, Filmfare Awards); and she wrote the dialogue for his acclaimed *Swami* (Lord and Master, 1977), based on Sharatchandra Chatterjee's Bengali novel of that title (1918). The relation of Rakesh's work to film followed the same pattern as Yadav's and Bhandari's fiction: parallel-cinema auteur Mani Kaul based *Uski roti* (official English title: His Food, 1970; later retitled Our Daily Bread) on one of Rakesh's short stories, and subsequently directed a film version of *Ashadh* (1971).

KAMLESHWAR PRASAD SAXENA (1932–2007) was educated at Allahabad University, and began his literary career in Allahabad, the city also associated with Upendranath Ashk (see above). He worked as an editor and freelance writer in the 1950s and 1960s, before moving to Bombay as the editor of the leading Hindi monthly, *Sarika* (1967–78), a position that Rakesh had held in 1962–63. While there, Kamleshwar also wrote extensively for the film industry: his most notable credits were *Aandhi* (The

Storm) and *Mausam* (The Weather), both box-office successes directed by Gulzar in 1975; the former was based on his novel *Kali aandhi* (The Black Storm), and the latter on a short story. As editor of *Sarika*, Kamleshwar strongly encouraged writers from oppressed and marginalized communities, particularly Marathi Dalits and Bohra Muslims, which brought new literatures to a large national audience in Hindi; as editor of *Hans*, Yadav later adopted a very similar stance but pushed it to a radical extreme, highlighting Hindi Dalit, Muslim, and especially women's writing in provocative, controversial ways.

Progressives and Modernists in Postcolonial Hindi Writing

Pragativad, 'progressivism', was more or less an organized movement in literature and the arts, which brought together writers, artists, intellectuals, performers, and theatre and film professionals from the early 1930s onward; their common bond was a commitment, in some measure, to Marxism, socialism, or communism. The literary movement therefore represented a wide spectrum of writers, from those on the far left (card-carrying members of the Communist Party of India or one of its offshoots) to those in moderate political positions (socialists of various hues, social democrats, and Nehruvian Fabian socialists), and on to those who were only 'fellow travellers'. The organized forms of *pragativad* were the All-India Progressive Writers' Association, launched in 1936 with Premchand as its first president, and the Indian People's Theatre Association, founded in 1943; both were closely related to transnational initiatives, with forerunners ranging from Indian Muslim expatriates in England to activist groups in Sri Lanka. A high proportion of the writers and artists now recognized as major figures in the postcolonial period for their innovation are aligned with progressive politics; and the movement in general has deeply influenced artistic and cultural practices across the subcontinent, down to the present.

Prayogavad, 'experimentalism', understood specifically as a face of modernism, was less organized in the public sphere, but also gathered momentum in the 1930s and 1940s across India, alongside the progressive movement. The primary locus of modernist experimentation was the group or coterie rather than the association, and its principal practitioner was the independent artist. However, the two movements blurred into each other from the beginning; Harish Trivedi has already pointed out the irony that five of the seven 'experimental modernists' included in Agyeya's pioneering *Tar saptak* (1943) anthology also identified themselves as 'Marxists' or 'communists'.[3] But this was not a confusion or contradiction: in Europe, the dialectic of progressive politics and aesthetic experimentation that unfolded in France with Charles Baudelaire and Arthur Rimbaud, for example, found a synthesis in the Bauhaus movement in Germany in the 1920s, for which modernism could be only progressive. In India, after Independence, the two movements tended towards greater mutual exclusion, so that the new story, novel, and poetry in various languages often distinguished themselves from their progressive counterparts by claiming to be articulations of apolitical modernist experimentation.

Rakesh viewed himself as an experimentalist, a modernist without a doctrinaire political agenda in the foreground; but he also saw himself as an artist fundamentally committed to representing the everyday lifeworld of ordinary men and women, specifically their experience of the realities of contemporary India, which were unprecedented and had never been depicted in its literature (for instance, the modernization of small towns, urban housing for individuals living alone, divorced women with children, middle-class ownership of cars, paperback books, transistor radios, and so on). His perspective on his progressive contemporaries simultaneously was—and was not—ambivalent. He was very close to Upendranath Ashk, who had become an icon of progressive realism in the late 1930s (see above); but he was deeply critical of writers on the far left, such as Yashpal and Ram Vilas Sharma, and many progressive writers, in turn, were inimical to his modernism. The three people he mentions in his diary entry of 6 February 1959 as being 'antagonistic' to *Ashadh* in Lucknow—Amritlal Nagar, Bhagavati Charan Verma, and Sarvadanand Verma— were writers on the left who would have viewed the play as an aesthetic experiment without satisfactory political moorings. But, in the earlier entry of 1 September 1958, Rakesh is delighted with the complimentary review by Namvar Singh, a more moderate progressive who was to become a remarkable theorist and scholar of the 'new' Hindi writing in the following decade.[4]

EXPLANATORY AND DRAMATURGICAL NOTES TO THE PLAY

The following notes do *not* include information on all seven of the Sanskrit poems and plays usually attributed to the historical Kalidas. For full information, see the English translations listed together under Kalidas in the Works Cited. However, some references to them in the dialogue are annotated below; five of the works are discussed in the Afterword; and the classical poet himself is covered more generally in the Introduction. The following notes also do not include any commentary on Rakesh's use of 'Sanskritized Hindi' in the dialogue; important aspects of the vocabulary, diction, and style, and their relation to the characters and characterization, are analysed in the Translators' Note and the Afterword.

Dramatis Personae

The names of all the characters in *Ashadh ka ek din* are derived from Sanskrit but, with the exception of Kalidas, they belong to fictional characters invented by Mohan Rakesh. The names are chosen carefully to communicate important personality traits, moral qualities, or conventional roles.

Ambika means 'mother' and 'good woman'—like the two other names, Amba and Ambalika, to which it is connected by etymology and in mythology. In the Mahabharata, the sisters Amba, Ambika, and Ambalika are princesses of Kashi (today's Banaras or Varanasi); the warrior and regent Bhishma abducts them as polygamous wives for his half-brother, Vichitravirya, but the latter dies before any children are conceived. Vichitravirya's other half-brother, Krishna Dvaipayana (who also reflexively happens to be the epic's author or redactor), is brought in to 'service' the three young widows, under the law of levirate; with Ambika, the middle wife, he fathers Dhritarashtra, the blind king who rules subsequently at Hastinapura, while his sons (the Kauravas) and nephews (the Pandavas) wage war over the division of the kingdom. In Rakesh's play, Ambika's abject condition as an ageing widow (and single mother) is ironically at variance with her mythical name and with her namesake's trajectory in the epic.

Mallika is the Sanskrit term for a variety of jasmine. Since the classical period, the whiteness, delicacy, and fragrance of the flower have made it a literary and artistic symbol of purity, innocence, vulnerability, and tenderness. Significantly, in the historical Kalidas's *The Recognition of Shakuntala*, the heroine Shakuntala nurtures a 'jasmine vine' (*nava-mallika*, a 'fresh offspring of jasmine') in her foster-father's grove; early in Act One, she fully identifies herself with that plant, a self-reflexive figure that comes to dominate the play's imagery. Shakuntala names the vine *vana-jyotsana*, 'the radiance of the forest'; as she observes, it wraps itself around an adjacent mango tree, so that vine and tree 'are twined in perfect harmony'[5]—a metaphor that Rakesh implicitly extends further in *Ashadh*.

Kalidas means 'the servant or slave of Kali', the fierce female deity in Hinduism who is an aspect of the goddess Durga, herself the terrifying aspect of the benign Parvati, consort of the god Shiva; more abstractly, the last two together represent the transcendent male and female principles of power (*shakti*) in the universe. Kali is associated with the colour black, with blackness and time, and with mortality and death; Shiva is an embodiment not only of destructive but also, equally, of creative power, and therefore is invoked constantly in the Indian arts. The elephant-headed god Ganesha is Shiva and Parvati's 'son' (the relationship is complex and ambivalent);

among other functions, Ganesha is the god of memory and intellect, and hence of knowledge and wisdom—he is the patron deity of writing, history, and literature, and hence of scribes and poets. Worshippers of any of these deities are connected to Shaivism, demographically the 'smaller' branch of Hinduism since classical times; historically, this branch is associated with the region 'south' of the Indo-Gangetic plain, around the Vindhya mountains and in the peninsula. In the case of the historical poet Kalidas, his name, his identification with Shaivism, the fact that the poems and plays ascribed to him carry verses invoking Shiva, and his legendary association with the ancient 'southern' city of Ujjayini (near the Vindhyas) mutually reinforce each other, probably circularly. Rakesh's fictional Kalidas overtly embodies creative power, memory, intellect, poetic wisdom, and the force of verbal composition; the play suppresses the religious elements in this mythology, but Act Three strongly suggests that Kalidas 'retires' in the end to Kashi, proverbially 'Shiva's city'.

Dantul comes from *danta* (cognate with English 'dental'), the Sanskrit word for 'tooth'; his name suggests that he 'has bite', and hence is combative or pugnacious, which are the main qualities he displays on stage.

Matul means 'maternal uncle'. He is literally a maternal uncle who adopts and raises the fictional Kalidas as his foster-son in the village, and serves as the young poet's head-of-household and next of kin. More generally, Matul is an avuncular presence in the community for younger characters such as Mallika and Nikshep (see discussion in Translators' Note).

Nikshep is a polysemic term with contradictory meanings. It designates the act of throwing away, abandoning, or renouncing something, as well as the act of placing, securing, or depositing. In the latter sense, it also denotes a deposit; something of value that is entrusted or assigned; a charge, trust, or guardianship. Nikshep's character invokes several of these shifting meanings in the course of the events on stage.

Vilom literally means 'an opposite, an adversary, a reverse, or contrary'; it designates an antonym (in language), an inverse (in mathematics), and an antagonist (in narrative). Vilom's character also matches the standard modern definitions of alter ego and doppelgänger. More than the other figures, he is a bundle of abstract qualities rather than an individual with a biography or a realistically represented personality; Rakesh conceives of him as a dramatic device, a three-dimensional contrivance who mobilizes particular conflicts and helps drive the action.

Rangini and *Sangini* are interchangeable young women who believe they have brought city 'culture' to the 'natural' environment of the village. Rakesh's text plays with the verbal origins of the two names, which grammatically carry feminine endings. *Ranga* means colour, but is also the general metaphor for vibrant, live performance; the common term for theatre in several Indian languages is *ranga-manch*, 'the performance stage', and the term for 'the field of theatre', as a domain of artistic practice, is *ranga-bhumi*. *Sanga* means companionship or togetherness. The Sanskrit *natak* or play frequently employs the device of a pair of female friends—

such as Anasuya and Priyamvada in the historical Kalidas's *The Recognition of Shakuntala*—who accompany a vulnerable heroine as supportive companions in public space. Rakesh inverts, satirizes, and hence defamiliarizes the classical convention: Rangini and Sangini intrude upon Mallika's domestic space and privacy as mock anti-companions, whose strangeness leaves her stupefied and estranged. Both young women are flat rather than round characters; their rhyming names signify a lack of individuality and an element of self-parody.

Anusvar and *Anunasik* are the male counterparts of Rangini and Sangini, with names that heighten the element of comedy and parody. Linguistically, in Sanskrit and the Indo-Aryan languages, the *anusvar* represents 'vowel nasality' (*n, ng, m,* etc.), the nasalization of a consonant–vowel combination (as in *ring, rung, rang* in English); in written form, it is a diacritical mark (a *bindu* or dot) placed above the nasalized letters. *Anunasik* means 'nasal, pronounced through the nose'; it is a variant of the *anusvar*, and is written as a *chandra-bindu* (horizontal crescent with superscript dot) above the nasalized combination. In Devanagari orthography, an *anusvar* and an *anunasik* replace each other under certain phonological and grammatical conditions, but represent exactly the same sound value in pronunciation. Rakesh exploits this arcane linguistic technicality with great relish in his characterization of the two men: they are completely interchangeable and indistinguishable bureaucratic ciphers who, metaphorically, do not achieve even the dignity of being stand-alone letters in the alphabet.

Priyangumanjari is a nominal compound in Sanskrit: *priyangu* denotes 'a vine that can blossom at the touch of a woman', and also 'saffron' (the dried stigmas of the saffron flower are used as a culinary spice and as a dyestuff); *manjari* is a cluster of buds and blossoms. The compound is thus a 'high' metaphor suitable for an imperial princess: it describes her as a bouquet of flowers on a vine blossoming in response to a delicate touch. Rakesh characterizes her ironically as a woman of artifice, who labours to match and counteract Mallika's effortless beauty and grace. The contrast between the two women mimics the verbal contrast between their names: both epithets evoke the loveliness and fragrance of flowers, but 'Priyangumanjari' is too ornate and unwieldy to achieve the immediacy of 'Mallika'.

Act One

Pages 83–84 (Opening stage direction)

Hindu swastika symbols. The word *swasti* in Sanskrit denotes approbation, health, and well-being; the ancient Hindu swastika is therefore an iconographic symbol that denotes auspiciousness and good fortune. The Nazis appropriated the graphic symbol for its high-cultural, almost mystical value in early Indo-Aryan society, rotated it by forty-five degrees, and produced one of the most fearful emblems of the twentieth century.

Vermilion. This is the closest English term to *geru*, a reddish pigment used for decorative purposes; in classical times, *gaura* (the original Sanskrit term) represents a range, from gold to

orange to vermilion. The colour is used in dyeing the robes
of ascetics, and hence is 'holy'.

Front door. In premodern India, a door had two panels that
opened inwards into a room. This should be kept in mind while
reading Rakesh's stage directions and while designing the set.

A door upstage left. This door to the inner room also has two
panels.

Clay lamps. A lamp of this kind is like a small, shallow bowl
(two to three inches in diameter and about an inch deep) made
of unglazed red clay; it is filled with seed oil; the lamp is used
by lighting a suitably sized, hand-rolled cotton wick, which
is soaked in the oil and is propped against and juts above the
bowl's edge. In modern Indian homes, such lamps are still
used during Diwali, the late-autumn Hindu 'festival of lights'.

Directors, production designers, set and lighting engineers,
and stage managers should note that the opening stage
direction for Act One does not mention a row of small clay
lamps along the front edge of the stage, and a bracket on the
wall of the main room to hold a flaming wooden torch safely.
When Vilom enters in this act, he lights these lamps with his
torch, which he then places in the bracket (see p. 111 of the
play-text).

Lotuses and conch shells. Both these are icons in classical Hindu
religious symbolism. Here the lotus also symbolizes beauty
in the midst of squalor, since it blooms above its lily pad in
the still and often dirty water of village ponds. The shells

are 'reminders' of the sacred aspects of marriage, since large conches are sounded at weddings and during worship at temples.

Wood-burning clay stove. About the size and shape of a large bucket or pail, this type of stove has a two-inch thick wall of hard clay; a round metal grate sits in the well, a few inches below the upper edge, on which small pieces of firewood (or coal in modern times) are piled and lit; a single, sizeable arched opening in the side, near the bottom, facilitates the removal of ash and cinders. This type of portable stove was common in urban Indian kitchens until the spread of modern stoves using natural gas in the 1970s, and continues to be used in villages. It is placed at ground level in a kitchen or outdoors, and requires women to cook while squatting on the ground or sitting on a low wooden stool.

Reed winnowing pan. A sturdy, square pan made of woven reeds, like wicker, with three edges turned up to contain the grain, and the fourth left flat for pouring it out. The grain is husked by rubbing between the palms, and the chaff is separated with circular and up-and-down motions of the pan (rather than by blowing on it).

Pages 85–86

Song. The lyrics are in Sanskrit, not Hindi; Rakesh may have taken them from a canonical source, or composed them himself. Verses about a traveller's loneliness on the road are common and conventional in Prakrit and classical Sanskrit poetry.

Page 89

Agnimitra. In this play, Agnimitra is a 'middleman' sent by Ambika to negotiate a possible match for Mallika, but he never appears on stage. Rakesh may be alluding to the historical Kalidas's play, *Malavikagnimitra* (Malavika and Agnimitra), but the reference has to be ironic because its namesake protagonist is a king. However, Rakesh's oblique joke is apt, because the classical comedy has go-betweens trying to arrange courtly liaisons and lovers' secret meetings right under the nose of the watchful queen.

Page 97

Ujjayini's royal court. Here and later, Rakesh uses the dialogue to suggest that, in the play's setting, the city of Ujjayini (presumably the same as the real city near the Vindhya mountains—see Map) is an imperial 'capital'. This mixes fiction with legend and history. Historically, Ujjayini in central India is a very ancient urban centre; it is associated with the Shakas who ruled west-central India during the first to third centuries; in the first decade of the fifth century, Chandragupta Vikramaditya (the historical Kalidas's supposed patron) drove out the Shakas, and made Ujjayini the 'capital' of the Gupta empire's western *province*; the imperial capital proper, however, remained at Pataliputra, about 800 km (500 miles) to the east. Independent of this political background, the classical poet Kalidas is very strongly associated with Ujjayini because *The Cloud-Messenger* contains a beautiful description of the city, suggesting that he knew it well, possibly as a resident. Rakesh draws on one set of legends about the historical author, which claim that he belonged to the region and became a court poet at a royal court in Ujjayini—which may or may not have been a part of the imperial order of the Gupta dynasty at that time.

'A Gathering of Seasons'. The Sanskrit title of this long descriptive poem, sometimes classified as an extended lyric, is *Ritusamhara* ('circle, round, or garland of the seasons'). The male speaker offers the description of six seasons to his beloved, as a gift in words to enchant her mind and senses. A model for numerous later poems on the same theme, the poem is often set to music and performed as a dance drama celebrating the beauty of the seasons and nature.

Acharya Vararuchi. An acharya is a learned man who is also in a position of authority. Since Kalidas is a poet and is being offered patronage, the royal court has sent an eminent scholar to invite and escort him to Ujjayini.

Page 102

Arya. Literally, an inhabitant of *Aryavarta*, an ancient name for India in the Vedic language. As a term of formal address in Sanskrit until classical times, it portrays the addressee as a 'well-born, honourable man'—though later works sometimes use it ironically. Here, Mallika uses it as term of respect for the avuncular Matul; later, she uses the same form of address for Vilom, but with the edge of forced formality in a state of anger.

Page 107

Matul's third eye. In Hindu myth, the god Shiva has a third eye located in the middle of his brow; it opens when he is in a rage or fury, and its 'eyebeam' destroys whatever it falls upon. Shiva's third eye thus embodies his fearsome divine power of destruction. Nikshep applies the metaphor of a 'third eye' to Matul ironically.

Temple of the goddess Jagdamba. 'Jagdamba' is another name for the goddess Durga or Kali. In his moment of crisis, Kalidas appropriately retreats into the temple on the mountain near the village dedicated to the goddess he worships.

Page 123

These clouds will travel towards Ujjayini. In the historical Kalidas's poem *The Cloud-Messenger*, the protagonist is a *yaksha* (a male celestial being or demigod), whose master Kubera, the Hindu god of wealth, punishes him for 'dereliction of duty' with twelve months of 'solitary confinement' on a mountain in central India. The *yaksha* is desperate to send a message explaining his imprisonment and absence to his beloved, a *yakshi* (a celestial female), who has been awaiting his return at their distant home in Alaka, Kubera's divine city in the Himalayas. Unable to resort to any other means of communication with her, the *yaksha* begs a passing raincloud in the sky to be his messenger, and gives it detailed instructions on how to reach his abode, and what to say to his beloved. As an essential stage in its itinerary, the cloud should travel first to nearby Ujjayini, and then head straight north to the Himalayas (see Map). Rakesh 'inverts' this enchanted tale, and has Mallika observe that the clouds gathered over the rainy village 'will travel towards Ujjayini' the next day, as though serving as her 'messengers of love' accompanying Kalidas to the capital—an inversion of *The Cloud-Messenger* at multiple levels.

Act Two

Page 124 (Opening stage direction)

Pages of bark manuscript and *blank book made of bark sheets*. Acts Two and Three of the play mention, and make extensive dramatic use of, two distinct sets of objects made from the bark of the *bhoja* tree and associated with writing. The first set consists of loose-leaf manuscripts of Kalidas's works that Mallika has obtained from the merchants of Ujjayini who pass through her village occasionally. Our translation refers to these consistently as 'manuscripts' or 'manuscript pages'. The second set consists of a single, bound, handmade 'volume', containing sheets of bark that Mallika herself has fashioned into pages and sewn together as a gift for Kalidas—a 'notebook' to write in, which she never gets to give him in Act Two. Since the sheets are blank, this is not yet a 'manuscript', and the translation distinguishes it clearly as the 'book' or 'blank book'.

Mortar. Made of heavy metal or polished stone, and of a handy size, it is dedicated to the grinding of small quantities of medicinal herbs and roots.

Page 131

'Mridanga' and 'veena'. The *mridanga* is a double-conical drum played with both hands; of classical origin, it is now a primary percussion instrument in the Carnatic style of music

in southern India. The *veena* is a seven-stringed, plucked instrument with a second resonance chamber made from a gourd. Traditionally associated with Saraswati, the goddess of knowledge, wisdom, and the arts, the *veena* has a deeper timbre than the sitar, which is said to have descended from it in post-classical times.

Page 144

Travel by a different route. Kalidas, Priyangumanjari, and their royal entourage are on their way from Ujjayini, in west-central India, to the region of Kashmir, in the far north. Priyangumanjari emphasizes that she decided to take a less convenient route because of her strong desire to visit Mallika and to see the region where Kalidas spent his childhood and youth. The Map included in this book offers a graphic analysis of the geographical 'triangle' defined by Ujjayini and Kashmir (which are real places) and the play's 'village' (which is imaginary, and the location of which is indeterminate); the Map also positions these three sites in relation to Kashi, the city to which the fictional Kalidas is supposed to 'retire', and for which, presumably, he departs at the end of Act Three.

Page 155

Indravarma and Vishnudutt. Probably two other courtiers in the royal entourage, who do not appear on stage. 'Indravarma', a warrior's name, means 'he who is protected by lord Indra' (Zeus's counterpart in the Vedic or ancient Hindu pantheon of gods); 'Vishnudutt', a merchant's or a banker's name, means 'he who is a gift of lord Vishnu' (the major Hindu god, counterpart of Shiva, whose worship increased greatly in the classical period).

Page 156

Demoness. Rakesh's term here is *rakshasi*. Ambika may be referring to a specific classical tale, but we have not been able to identify it.

Act Three

Page 166

Kashi. The oldest and most sacred of the cities of Hinduism, it is usually called 'Shiva's city'; it stands on the River Ganga in north-central India, in the 'Hindi heartland' on the Indo-Gangetic plain (see Map). Also called Banaras and Varanasi in post-classical and modern times, its historical foundations are probably more than 2500 years old; in Hindu mythology, however, it is said to be much older. Since at least the fourth century (the beginning of the classical period), it has been the premier destination for pilgrimage among Hindus; the place to seek 'purification' and Shiva's 'grace', and to purify oneself in the river's holy waters; and the city to seek out at the end of one's life, for a passage to God or 'heaven'. Since many Hindus wish to be cremated in Kashi, and to have their ashes scattered in the river, the city has many ancient cremation sites along the riverfront. In the case of Kalidas, 'the servant or slave of Kali' (Shiva's consort), the mention of Kashi brings this full range of classical–modern associations into play for Indian readers and viewers.

Page 177

The Origin of the Young God. . . . This passage, which mentions several Sanskrit works by the historical Kalidas, is a turning point in the play and its meanings; it is annotated and explained in the Afterword. For the works themselves, see the translations listed under Kalidas in the Works Cited.

Page 182

Ashtavakra. Literally, 'the one with eight crooked limbs'; in Sanskrit, the name of an ancient sage's son who was born with extreme deformities, and whose story is narrated in the Mahabharata. Rakesh gives the name satirically to the local astrologer or diviner in the village, who—like Agnimitra, Acharya Varuruchi, and Indravarma and Vishnudutt—does not appear on stage.

Endnotes

Introduction

1. See *Mohan rakesh ke sampurna natak* (The Complete Plays of Mohan Rakesh, hereafter *CP*), pp. 5–8; and Taneja, *Mohan rakesh*, pp. 29–31.

2. See Blackwell and Kumar, 'Mohan Rakesh's *Lahrom ke rajhams*'; Chandra, *Mohan Rakesh's* Halfway House; interview to Coppola; Dalmia, 'Neither Half nor Whole'; A. Dharwadker, *Theatres of Independence*, pp. 225–43 and passim, and 'Mohan Rakesh, Modernism'; Meisig, 'Kalidas's Life and Works'; Sawhney, *The Modernity of Sanskrit*; and Thakur, *Mohan Rakesh's* Ashadh ka ek din.

3. A. Dharwadker, *Theatres of Independence*, p. 226.

4. For a full discussion see A. Dharwadker, *Theatres of Independence*, pp. 225–28.

5. See Figuera, *Translating the Orient*, pp. 12–13 and 190–91.

6. Rakesh, *Bakalam khud* (With My Own Pen, hereafter *BK*), pp. 93–94. All translations from Hindi in this Introduction are mine.

7. *CP*, p. 196; for a full translation of this preface, see Appendix 5.

8. Ibid., p. 197; see further analysis in Afterword.

9. Ibid., pp. 196–98.

10. Ibid., p. 196.

11. Interview to Coppola, p. 32.

12. Ibid., p. 33.

13. Rakesh, 'Looking Around as a Playwright', pp. 18–19.

14. Ibid., p. 19.

15. Eliot, 'Tradition and Individual Talent', p. 2320.

16. *CP*, p. 197.

17. See Miller, *Theater of Memory*, pp. 3–5 and 315.

18. Interview to Coppola, p. 32.

19. *CP*, p. 110.

20. Interview to Coppola, p. 26.

21. *CP*, p. 106; for an alternative translation (by Vinay Dharwadker), see Appendix 1.

22. Ibid.

23. Interview to Coppola, p. 30.

24. Introduction to Rushdie and West, eds, *Mirrorwork*, p.vii.

25. *CP*, p. 104.

26. *Natya-vimarsha* (Reflections on Theatre, hereafter *NV*), p. 38.

27. Ibid., p. 37.

28. Ibid., p. 38.

29. Ibid., p. 44.

30. *BK*, p. 109.

31. *CP*, p. 105.

32. See *CP*, pp. 206–19.

33. *NV*, p. 46.

34. Rakesh, 'Looking Around as a Playwright', p. 18.

35. *NV*, p. 65.

36. Rakesh, 'Theatre without Walls', p. 67.

37. Ibid.

38. Grotowski, 'I Said Yes to the Past', p. 81.

39. Dubey, 'Rakesh'.

40. *CP*, p. 120.

41. Dubey, 'Rakesh'.

42. See Taneja, *Mohan rakesh*, pp. 60–156.

43. Quoted in Taneja, *Mohan rakesh*, p. 62.

44. *CP*, p. 114.

45. Ibid., pp. 109–10.

46. Ibid., p. 115.

47. Ibid., p. 116.

48. Quoted in Taneja, *Mohan rakesh*, pp. 61 and 68.

49. Dubey, 'Rakesh'.

50. *CP*, p. 112.

Translators' Note

1. See Appendix 4.

2. For a full discussion, see V. Dharwadker, 'Ramanujan'; for other theorists, see Schulte and Biguenet, eds, *Theories of Translation*.

3. Schulte and Biguenet, eds, *Theories of Translation*, p. 17; V. Dharwadker, 'Ramanujan', p. 116.

4. See *CP*, pp. 28–36.

5. Aristotle, *Poetics*, p. 53.

6. See V. Dharwadker, 'Ramanujan', pp. 126–30. For Derrida, the 'syntagmatic level' of a text is the domain of its syntax or sentence-structure, which uses the logic of metonymy or association to string words together in a sequence. He contrasts it with the 'paradigmatic level' of a text, which is the domain of word choice and uses the logic of metaphor or substitutability. (On metaphor and metonymy, see Note 8 below.) Derrida argues that the translation of a sentence from one language to another is shaped primarily by the specific word choices that a translator makes in order to fill the word positions dictated by the syntax of the second language. This leaves translation open to 'allegoresis', which is the inverse of the process of constructing an allegory. When a poet composes an allegory, she uses a concrete image to represent an abstract idea, or a personification to represent a concept or an argument; when a

translator practises allegoresis, she renders concrete images in the original language with abstract 'equivalents' in the language of the translation. As commentator and translator, Derrida himself prefers the 'paradigmatic' mode of allegoresis, which allows him to substitute the 'concrete' words in an original with their 'abstract equivalents' in a translation.

7. Bakhtin, *Dialogic Imagination*, pp. 426–28.

8. An explication of this point may be useful. A *simile* asserts that some object X is *like* a different object Y; for example, the sentence 'Her face is like the moon' is a simile, and its basis is a relation of similarity between 'face' and 'moon', even though the two things remain distinct because of some underlying differences between them. When the similarity between X and Y is comprehensive, and there is no underlying difference to distinguish them, a simile becomes a *metaphor*: 'Her face *is* the moon.' A metaphor usually asserts that two objects X and Y are identical, mutually substitutable, or analogous. In a *metonymy*, an object X represents or *stands for* another object Y, not because they are necessarily similar, identical, mutually substitutable, or analogous, but simply because X and Y are *associated* with each other. Thus, 'She wears pearls' is a metonymy, in which the word 'pearls' stands for a necklace made of pearls, and we understand the sentence to mean that 'She wears (a necklace of) pearls'. If the association between X and Y in a metonymy is that between a member (X) of a class and the class itself (Y), then usually there is some similarity between X and the other members of the class Y; if all the members of the class are identical, then X has a double relationship to Y of identity as well as association by membership; and if X is made to stand for Y under this condition, then X becomes a *metonymous metaphor* for Y. For instance, if all the pearls in a necklace are identical (as in a necklace of cultured pearls), then 'She wears pearls' contains a metonymous metaphor.

In an antiparallel metonymy, an object (X) may be associated with a class of objects (Y) that are its opposites or contraries. In the example from the first part of Rakesh's sentence discussed here, 'a single flaw' is associated with 'a crowd of virtues', and the flaw hides among (and becomes a member of a class of) its opposites—and hence is an antiparallel metonymy. The metonymy in the second part is 'the moon's blemish hides itself in a multitude of rays'; like the metonymy in the first, this is also an antiparallel structure, because 'blemish' and 'rays' are contraries. But the process of 'hiding' may be different in these two parts of the sentence. A flaw that is hidden in a crowd of virtues may not be visible at all; whereas the moon's blemish always remains visible, though it may be rendered insignificant by the moon's rays. Thus, the 'internal logic' of the two antiparallel metonymies in the sentence is different because of the different ways in which the 'hiding' may occur in the two cases.

The phrase 'just as' between the first two parts of the quoted sentence creates an analogy or equation between them. The first two parts of the sentence together, therefore, constitute an extended metonymous metaphor, with 'just as' establishing a metaphorical identity between two antiparallel metonymies with divergent forms of internal logic. But the third and final part of the sentence (after the dash) then introduces a 'broken metonym' because, unlike 'flaw' and 'blemish' in the first two parts, 'destitution' is not associated with a class of objects in which it might hide itself. By omitting an equivalent of 'a crowd of virtues' and 'a multitude of rays' in the third part, Rakesh deliberately leaves his extended figurative structure incomplete, expecting his audience to contemplate the possibilities on their own. Mallika's comment on 'destitution' thus becomes irrefutable because she does not tell us where it 'hides' itself, or how—the unfinished metonymy omits the basis on which a disagreement might be formulated.

9. Aristotle, *Poetics*, p. 104.

10. Ibid., pp. 67 and 73–79.

11. V. Dharwadker, 'Ramanujan', pp. 120–23.

12. See Appendix 3.

Afterword

1. Taneja, *Mohan rakesh*, p. 45.

2. See Appendix 5.

3. See Dällenbach, *The Mirror in the Text*.

4. Monegal and Reid, eds, *Borges: A Reader*.

5. Ibid., p. 99; emphasis in original.

6. Ibid., p. 159.

7. Ibid., p. 161.

8. Ibid.

9. See van Buitenen, trans., *The Mahabharata*, pp. 723–60.

10. See Kalidas in Works Cited; and Thapar, *Sakuntala*.

11. See, especially, Aristotle, *Poetics*.

12. Ramanujan, *Collected Essays*, p. 163.

13. Hobson, *Derrida*, p. 75.

14. Ibid., p. 78.

15. Baudelaire, *Flowers of Evil*, pp. 16–19.

16. Joyce, *Portrait of the Artist*, p. 189; and Yeats, *Collected Poems*, pp. 336–37.

17. King, ed., *Long Day's Journey* (O'Neill), p. 181.

18. See Introduction, Chronology, and Notes.

19. See Appendix 4.

20. See Appendix 6.

21. Puchner, *Stage Fright*, pp. 22–28.

22. A. Dharwadker, *Theatres of Independence*, pp. 157–60.

23. Wolpert, *New History*, pp. 88–94.

24. Bakhtin, *Dialogic Imagination*, p. 84.

25. Ibid., pp. 131–36.

26. Eliot, 'Tradition and the Individual Talent', p. 2320.
27. Joyce, *Portrait of the Artist*, p. 186.

Appendices

1. Translated from *CP*, p. 104.
2. Ibid., p. 105.
3. Translated from *Punashcha*, pp. 88–89.
4. Translated from *CP*, pp. 196–98.
5. Ibid., pp. 201–02.

Notes

1. See Appendix 5.
2. See Appendix 4.
3. Trivedi, 'The Progress of Hindi, Part 2', p. 998.
4. See Appendix 1.
5. Kalidas, *Abhijnana-shakuntala*, 'Sakuntala and the Ring of Recollection', Miller, trans., p. 95.

Works Cited

The works cited in our commentary are listed below in the Modern Language Association bibliographic style, adapted as necessary. Some entries are annotated in order to identify particular content in the source. *Mohan rakesh ke sampurna natak* (The Complete Plays of Mohan Rakesh), mentioned here under the author's name, has been sometimes cited in the book as *CP*. Under Kalidas, each of the seven works usually attributed to him is identified by: Sanskrit title; English translation of title, as used in this book; and bibliographic details of a standard modern translation of the work. See the Chronology for information on additional works by and about Rakesh, which do not reappear here because they are not cited in our commentary.

Anouilh, Jean. *Five Plays*. Vol. 1. New York: Noonday Press, 1990. [Includes *Antigone*: 1–53; *Eurydice*: 55–120.]

Aristotle. *On Rhetoric: A Theory of Civil Discourse*. Trans. and ed. George A. Kennedy. 2nd ed. New York: Oxford University Press, 2007.

———. *The Poetics*. Trans. Stephen Halliwell. Loeb Classical Library. Cambridge, Massachusetts: Harvard University Press, 1995.

Bakhtin, M.M. *The Dialogic Imagination: Four Essays*. Ed. Michael Holquist. Trans. Caryl Emerson and Michael Holquist. Austin, Texas: University of Texas Press, 1981.

Baudelaire, Charles. *The Flowers of Evil & Paris Spleen*. Trans. William H. Crosby. Introd. Anna Balakian. Brockport, New York: BOA Editions, 1991.

Beckett, Samuel. *Breath*. http://www.bradcoubourne.com/breath.txt. Accessed 1 August 2014.

———. *Endgame*. In Greenblatt, *Norton Anthology of English Literature*: 2393–2420.

Blackwell, Fritz, and Prem Kumar. 'Mohan Rakesh's *Lahrom ke rajhams* and Ashvaghosha's *Saundarananda*'. *Journal of South Asian Literature* 13.1–4 (1977): 45–52.

Chandra, Subhash. *Mohan Rakesh's* Halfway House: *Critical Perspectives*. New Delhi: Asia Book Club, 2001.

Conrad, Joseph. *Heart of Darkness*. Norton Critical Edition. 3rd ed. Ed. Robert Kimbrough. New York: W.W. Norton, 1988.

Coppola, Carlo. 'Mohan Rakesh' [interview]. *Journal of South Asian Literature* 9.2–3 (1973): 15–45.

Dällenbach, Lucien. *The Mirror in the Text*. Chicago: University of Chicago Press, 1989.

Dalmia, Vasudha. 'Neither Half nor Whole: Mohan Rakesh and the Modernist Quest'. *Poetics, Plays, and Performances: The Politics of Modern Indian Theatre*. New Delhi: Oxford University Press, 2006: 117–49.

Dharwadker, Aparna Bhargava. 'Mohan Rakesh, Modernism, and the Postcolonial Present'. *South Central Review* 25.1 (2008): 136–62.

———. *Theatres of Independence: Drama, Theory, and Urban Performance in India since 1947*. Iowa City: University of Iowa Press, 2005; New Delhi: Oxford University Press, 2006.

Dharwadker, Vinay. 'A.K. Ramanujan's Theory and Practice of Translation.' In *Post-colonial Translation: Theory and Practice*.

Ed. Susan Bassnett and Harish Trivedi. London: Routledge, 1999: 114–40.

Dubey, Satyadev. 'Rakesh'. *Enact* 73–74 (1973): n.p.

Eliot, T.S. 'Tradition and the Individual Talent' (1919). In Greenblatt, *Norton Anthology of English Literature*: 2319–25.

Figuera, Dorothy Matilda. *Translating the Orient: The Reception of Sakuntala in Nineteenth-Century Europe*. Albany: State University of New York Press, 1991.

Greenblatt, Stephen. Gen. ed. *The Norton Anthology of English Literature*. 8th ed. Vol. 2. New York: W.W. Norton, 2006.

Grotowski, Jerzy. 'I Said Yes to the Past' [Interview with Margaret Croyden]. In *The Grotowski Sourcebook*. Ed. Richard Schechner and Lisa Wolford. London: Routledge, 1997.

Hobson, Marian. *Jacques Derrida: Opening Lines*. New York: Routledge, 1998.

Joyce, James. *A Portrait of the Artist as a Young Man*. Norton Critical Edition. Ed. John Paul Riquelme. New York: W.W. Norton, 2007.

Kalidas. *Abhijnana-shakuntala* (The Recognition of Shakuntala). 'Sakuntala and the Ring of Recollection'. Trans. Barbara Stoller Miller. In Miller, *Theater of Memory*: 85–176.

———. *Kumara-sambhava* (The Origin of the Young God). *Kumarasambhavam: The Origin of the Young God*. Trans. Hank Heifetz. University of California Press, 1985; Gurgaon, Haryana: Penguin, 2014.

———. *Malavikagnimitram* (Malavika and Agnimitra). 'Malavika and Agnimitra'. Trans. Edwin Gerow. In Miller, *Theater of Memory*: 253–312.

———. *Meghaduta* (The Cloud-Messenger). *The Transport of Love: The Meghaduta of Kalidasa*. Trans. and introd. Leonard Nathan. Berkeley, California: University of California Press, 1976.

———. *Raghuvamsha* (Raghu's Dynasty). 'The Dynasty of Raghu'. Trans. Arthur W. Ryder. *Kalidasa: Translations of Shakuntala and Other Works*. London: J.M. Dent, 1912.

————. *Ritusamhara* (A Gathering of Seasons). 'Rtusamharam'. *Kalidasa: The Loom of Time: A Selection of His Plays and Poems.* Trans. and introd. Chandra Rajan. Penguin Classics. New Delhi: Penguin, 1989: 103–34.

————. *Vikramorvashiya* (Vikram and Urvashi). 'Urvasi Won by Valor'. Trans. David Gitomer. In Miller, *Theater of Memory*: 177–251.

Karnad, Girish. *Tughlaq*. Trans. Girish Karnad. New Delhi: Oxford University Press, 2014. [Orig. Kannada, 1964; English trans., 1972; this ed. with commentary by Karnad: ix–xxi, U.R. Anantha Murthy: xxv–xxvii, Aparna Dharwadker: 87–116.]

Meisig, Konrad. 'Kalidas's Life and Works as Reflected in Mohan Rakesh's Play *Ashadh ka ek din*'. In *Tender Ironies*. Ed. Dilip Chitre, et al. New Delhi: Manohar, 1994: 286–307.

Miller, Barbara Stoller, ed. *Theater of Memory: The Plays of Kalidasa.* New York: Columbia University Press, 1984.

Monegal, Emir Rodriguez, and Alastair Reid. Eds. *Borges: A Reader. A Selection from the Writings of Jorge Luis Borges.* New York: E.P. Dutton, 1981. [Includes 'Pierre Menard, Author of the Quixote', trans. Anthony Bonner: 96–103; 'The Aleph', trans. N.T. di Giovanni: 154 –63.]

O'Neill, Eugene. *Long Day's Journey into Night*. Critical Edition. Ed. William Davies King. New Haven, Connecticut: Yale University Press, 2014.

Puchner, Martin. *Stage Fright: Modernism, Anti-Theatricality, and Drama.* Baltimore: Johns Hopkins Press, 2002.

Rakesh, Mohan. *Bakalam khud* (With My Own Pen). Delhi: Rajpal, 1974.

————. 'Looking Around as a Playwright'. *Sangeet Natak 3* (October 1966): 16–21.

————. *Mohan rakesh ki dayari* (The Diary of Mohan Rakesh). Delhi: Rajpal, 1985.

————. *Mohan rakesh ke sampurna natak* (The Complete Plays of

Mohan Rakesh). Ed. Nemichandra Jain. Delhi: Rajpal, 1993.

———. *Natya-vimarsha* (Reflections on Theatre). Ed. Jaidev Taneja. New Delhi: National School of Drama, 2003.

———. *Punashcha: mohan rakesh aur ashk dampati ka patrachar* (Postscript: The Correspondence between Mohan Rakesh and the Ashk Couple). Ed. Jaidev Taneja. Delhi: Radhakrishna, 2000.

———. 'Theatre without Walls'. *Sangeet Natak* 6 (October–December 1967): 66–69.

Ramanujan, A.K. *The Collected Essays of A K. Ramanujan.* Gen. ed. Vinay Dharwadker. New Delhi: Oxford University Press, 1999.

Rushdie, Salman. 'Introduction'. *Mirrorwork: 50 Years of Indian Writing, 1947–1997.* Eds. Salman Rushdie and Elizabeth West. New York: Henry Holt, 1997: vii–xx.

Sawhney, Simona. *The Modernity of Sanskrit.* Minneapolis: University of Minnesota Press, 2009.

Schulte, Rainer, and John Biguenet. Eds. *Theories of Translation: An Anthology of Essays from Dryden to Derrida.* Chicago: University of Chicago Press, 1992. [Includes texts by John Dryden: 17–31; Walter Benjamin: 71–82; Paul Valéry: 113–26; Jacques Derrida: 218–27.]

Shaw, George Bernard. *Mrs Warren's Profession.* In Greenblatt, *Norton Anthology of English Literature*: 1743–89.

———. *Saint Joan: A Chronicle Play in Six Scenes and an Epilogue.* Penguin Classics. London: Penguin, 2003.

Taneja, Jaidev. *Mohan rakesh: rang-shilpa aur pradarshan* (Mohan Rakesh: Theatrecraft and Presentation). New Delhi: Radhakrishna Prakashan, 1996.

Thakur, N.C. *Mohan Rakesh's Ashadh ka ek din: A Critical Monograph.* New Delhi: Intellectual Book Corner, 1978.

Thapar, Romila. *Sakuntala: Texts, Readings, Histories.* New York: Columbia University Press, 2010.

Trivedi, Harish. 'The Progress of Hindi, Part 2: Hindi and the Nation'. In *Literary Cultures in History: Reconstructions from South*

Asia. Ed. Sheldon Pollock. Berkeley, California: University of California Press, 2003: 958–1022.

van Buitenen, J.A.B. Trans. and ed. *The Mahabharata*. Vol. 2. Chicago: University of Chicago Press, 1975.

Wolpert, Stanley. *A New History of India*. 4th ed. New York: Oxford University Press, 1993.

Yeats, W.B. *The Collected Poems of W.B. Yeats*. Revised 2nd ed. Ed. Richard J. Finneran. New York: Simon and Schuster, 1996.

Copyright Notice for Theatre Practitioners

Aparna Dharwadker and Vinay Dharwadker retain the world rights to any production or public performance of *One Day in the Season of Rain*, in whole or in part, in any medium or form, in this authorized English translation or in any translation or adaptation of this text into another language, by any amateur group or professional company. For written permission, interested individuals and groups should contact Aparna Dharwadker at adharwadker@wisc.edu and Vinay Dharwadker at vdharwadker@wisc.edu by email; or by writing to them at 7625 Farmington Way, Madison, Wisconsin 53717, or by fax at (608) 833-1451 in the USA.